Maritime Academy Graduate

Maritime Academy Graduate

~

Memoir Of A Third Mate

By

Mark H. Glissmeyer

Gradina Books

This book is a nautical memoir that describes my experiences aboard various merchant ships, so grab a handrail and come aboard. Experience what it was like to graduate and sail as a third mate in the late 1980's.

Gradina Books

ISBN-13: 978-0-9985416-3-1

This memoir is dedicated to the U.S. merchant sailors who were lost at sea during World War II. Their sacrifice and bravery will never be forgotten.

Contents

~

0

Anchor's Away

It was a beautiful winter day in 1984, and we were sailing down the Columbia River from Portland aboard our training ship, the Golden Bear. I was sitting up forward on number two hatch, admiring this scene after having just finished eating lunch in the mess with my fellow cadets. My head was still feeling the effects from the prior night—some of us had gone ashore and walked along the deserted waterfront looking for some amusement. There were abandoned warehouses and docks all along that stretch of the Willamette River where our ship was tied up, but we eventually found a bar down the way and had some drinks inside. I loved the whiskey sours they served, and kept drinking until the bartender refused to serve me anymore. I'd also gotten the address of a beautiful co-ed we met, she was going to nursing school and wanted me to write to her.

Eventually we went back to the ship and I slept it off, being back to normal duties the next day. So here I was still feeling the effects while noticing how fast the ship was going downstream—it was due to the current in the river. If we'd been headed upstream then we could safely go slower while maintaining steerage, but when going downstream we had to go faster to adjust for the extra speed of the river water.

The training ship was fairly old, having been built in 1940 during the onset of World War II, and precautions were normally made in case something went wrong. You'd never guess it's going to happen though, but then it does, and suddenly I hear the sound of the forward anchor windlass. There was a loud splash like they'd let go an anchor, and the windlass started to make a very loud rumble like it had anchor chain running out. I immediately thought that's impossible with the speed of the ship, who'd drop an anchor when we're moving this fast?

Then I noticed the ship starting to veer to starboard. It was slow, but sure enough, we were headed for the bank of the river. We must have lost the steering hydraulics!

I got up off the hatch cover and went forward towards the bow to see what was happening, and as I got closer, there was a mas - sive cloud of dust and sparks surrounding the anchor windlass as it spun like a top, with the anchor chain flying over it and out through the hawse pipe. A cadet was at the brake wheel trying to slow the speed of the ship, and the sparks were flying all over him and the other cadets surrounding him. The sound that the chain made as it left the hawse pipe was deafening.

I stopped near the ladder and didn't walk any closer, for fear something was about to happen. The anchor windlass itself was free-wheeling and producing smoke clouds and sparks from the brake. The chain coming out of the chain locker below was screaming out, and hopefully wasn't kinked when stored. Other- wise, it might be pulled out through the deck and even kill them upon coming back out and snapping in half.

I definitely didn't want to breathe any of that dust cloud, which consisted of flying rust from the chain, and sparks from the metal parts hitting together at an amazing speed. I couldn't believe how fast that chain was flying by over the windlass. From my own experiences with having painted the anchor chain, I knew the early links nearest to the anchor were always black, and when we got closer to the last links—they were painted white. The very last ones were painted red as a warning that we were about to run out of chain.

As the ship had veered completely to starboard, this dust cloud and noise got worse in what seemed like the fastest minute of my life, until I saw the white links come up and pass over through the hawse pipe. They were nearing the end of the chain! The ship was now pointed straight at the river bank and was very close to hit- ting shore. Then the red links came up and started to pass over the windlass, what's going to happen when they hit the end?

The ship had slowed somewhat as I assumed they'd put her in full reverse by this point. But she had enough speed that nothing was going to stop the ship in time. And then the anchor chain ran out!

I had worked down in the chain locker during maintenance duties before and had seen how the chain was stored inside. There was an opening where we could inspect the chain after raising either anchor to see if it had any kinks in it. We could even see how the last link was connected to the bulkhead by a large pin. That pin was meant to snap away if the chain got taken out to the end so it wouldn't pull the bulkhead in. I'd noticed that the bulkhead was slightly bulging in though, so they must have hit the end at least a couple of times before without the pin breaking.

Anyway, this time everyone got lucky. There's no way that any thin bulkhead along with a link of chain could stop the moving weight of this ship. Instead, as the end of the last red link was reached, the pin holding it broke cleanly away. *What a miracle!* The cadets all stood there in shock as the final red link flew by and disappeared as it went out through the hawse pipe and down into the water. They couldn't believe what had just happened! And neither could I.

The dust cloud surrounding the area moved away, which left a heavy covering of chain rust all over the anchor windlass, the entire focsle, and all over the cadets themselves. The one that applied the brake removed his goggles to show a perfect silhouette of his eye sockets. A moment later we felt the ship hit the river bank, and she slid upon it and stopped. We were aground!

Luckily, nobody was killed in the process.

Actually, being grounded on the bank turned out to be a good thing, as we had no steering. We only had one anchor left obviously, having just lost the other one with all of its attached chain. So there we stayed, until they got the steering hydraulics working again. This was accomplished in about fifteen minutes, and they tested it to be sure things were working properly. Then the engines went full reverse and we eventually backed off from the bank of the river, and went out into the channel again. We managed to make it safely down the rest of the river on the way out, but with one less anchor to show for it. And no casualties except for some rusty cadets with a story to tell.

1

At The Academy

There were so many experiences like losing that anchor during my time at sea, that I probably should go back to the beginning. It's important because I never knew what the Merchant Marine was before attending the California Maritime Academy, and probably like most people, I'd have guessed it had to do with the military. But soon enough I'd learn what it meant, and that took place because of a chance encounter that happened ashore.

It all started when my father met a seaman in a bar who bragged about how wonderful life was at sea. He talked about his long vacations while only working half the year, and even mentioned how much money he made. It must have all sounded wonderful after a couple of drinks. So later I found out after graduating from high school in 1981 that I'd be going to a maritime academy. No one in my family knew it, but the maritime industry at that time was at an all-time low, and there wouldn't be many signs of improvement for some time to come.

The maritime academy my father picked out for me was on the West Coast of the United States in Vallejo, California, with the campus tucked into the straits by San Pablo Bay. It was a private academy at the time with two separate paths to go to sea. One was through the deck department (N.I.T.), and the other was through engineering (M.E.T.). I made the romantic choice and picked to go with the deck program.

It was four years to graduate for those with no prior credits, but allowed in transfer students that had taken general education classes and received credit for them to enter as a sophomore. In the deck division there were four groups; 1-D, 2-D, 3-D and 4-D. Upon arrival, I was placed in 2-D along with other students who came from various backgrounds. One had a father who sailed, another enjoyed racing sailboats, but mostly we all came from families who just picked this academy seemingly by random. With barely one of us coming from seafaring lineage, we'd be a new generation of sailors, and our hopes were high!

The academy itself was a nice campus that had dormitories, school buildings, a cafeteria, library and a snack shop. It was co-ed, so they had one section of the dormitories for the female cadets, and the rest were for the males. The training ship was moored at the academy's dock while not out on a cruise, and we had classes that kept up the maintenance on her. During the first week after my arrival, which was officially called *Indoctrination Week*, we had to get our hair cut, purchase the proper uniforms, and get the books we needed for classes. We were also assigned sleeping quarters in the old residence hall at the top of the hill. There was also some testing we were given for English class placement, something I'd found out about too late.

Next we were instructed on how to stand watches on campus as though we were out to sea. There was a cadet on watch at the front gate of the academy, a lookout in the upper parking lot, one who patrolled around the campus in an old jeep, and a watch out on the training ship. We did this while wearing a uniform of khakis with shiny black shoes and a CMA cap. Each cadet had bars on the collar to signify which class of cadet we were. These were purchased out of the academy through the clothing store.

We were also assigned cleaning duties with the newest cadets like myself, or fourth-class, doing all of the dirty work, while the third-class got to supervise us, at least while on campus. Demerits were handed out if we didn't do a good job of cleaning. We had cleaning assignments for the many stairs, bathrooms, hallways, and even our own bedrooms. We quickly learned how we were to become the janitors of the academy, and we were paying for the privilege.

In order to be sure that we kept up with our cleaning assignments and attire, a demerit system was enforced by the academy. Any cadet could get five or ten demerits if we failed to clean a job properly. After receiving the first demerits, if we failed to fix the offense—we'd get fifteen more. If we failed again, we'd get twenty-five more. At seventy-five they'd officially kick us out of school.

There was a rumor of one guy who'd received over seventy-five demerits recently and had been kicked out. He tried suing the academy to get back in, but was denied an appeal by the local court system. I even came close to getting kicked out myself, but more about that later.

All of the cadets who attended the academy were required to live on campus, and the first-year students stayed in the large building at the top of the stairs. It was sort of a long three-story brick building with a single aisle from end to end on each floor. There were sleeping quarters in most of the rooms which held two students each, and a communal bathroom and shower on each floor where we had little privacy. These areas were cleaned and inspected by the cadets, and were generally well kept throughout the year. The doors to each room were made of steel, and were very noisy to open and close. Many times I was awakened by someone leaving their room, whether it was for a watch at 4:00 a.m.—or just to use the bathroom at midnight.

An interesting thing about those steel doors was they were also used to administer punishment by fellow students. Every now and then we'd see someone locked in their room by revengeful cadets. They would use a broomstick across the door frame and tie the door handle with a rope to keep it from opening. Thus, anyone couldn't get out who was still inside. After an hour or two this was generally untied, and the offending student was allowed to leave again.

For the first two years we were scheduled to take mostly general education classes, with about half of those related to the maritime field. During my first semester my grades were pretty horrible as I adjusted to this situation. It was funny because even though this wasn't suppose to be a military occupation, it was mainly treated that way at the academy. Somehow I was still wondering if this industry should be my life-long ambition. Maybe in my mind, I thought if I did badly enough, I could leave it, but eventually it kicked in that this was to become a part of my life. And that happened after I got my grades back for the first semester, and saw the fruits of my labor.

I did well in Seamanship with an A, got a B in Shipboard Laboratory (that's shorthand for cleaning work aboard the training ship), a B in Math, and C's in Naval Science and Macro-Economics. I got a Pass in bonehead English and Boat Handling, which reminds me of how much I disliked that bonehead English class. That was assigned to those who did poorly on the entrance exam they'd given us during *Indoctrination Week*. Since the class was either pass or fail, I ended up writing obscure stories at the end just to finish it. My favorite assignment I handed in was the one about chopping down a tree using various methods. The story was hideous enough that our teacher, an English Major, realized I must've been kidding and gave it a D-, which was still a passing grade. Mission accomplished.

After the first semester, all the upper class left on the Golden Bear for their yearly training cruise. Since only the first, second and third-class cadets were allowed to sail aboard her, we stayed behind and took more general education classes. This was my favorite time on campus, since it meant as fourth-class cadets—we had the campus all to ourselves. No more bosses around to give us demerits; we got to run the campus as we wanted. Nobody was around to bully us, we were in charge of everything. Even the head commandant had left on the cruise. While my heart still wasn't entirely in this yet, I liked the fact it was more like a school and not some military camp, even if it lasted for only one semester.

It was the head commandant who was tasked with the responsibility of discipline at the academy. He would inspect all the students when we first arrived from semester breaks for haircuts and clothing, then weekly thereafter, and also handled all matters involving demerits. He always wore the school uniform around campus, as did the deck department instructors who taught us various classes during the week. The only ones in civilian clothes were those who worked in the administration building, and instructors who came in to teach a single class or general education.

One interesting class during my second semester was Calculus I. On the first day we had so many cadets attending that we were pulling chairs into the classroom from other areas just to make enough seats for us all. The chosen instructor seemed extremely intelligent, having the appearance of someone who should be in a lab somewhere doing photon experiments. After we got back the results of our first open book exam—his grading was very difficult on us. He'd even flunked half the class on the very first test! Some of the students got such low grades that they decided to drop out of the class, and after the second exam—even more dropped out, and then more after the third test.

By the end of the semester—which had started with around forty-five students—we finished with a small group of ten of us in a semi-circle watching him up at the chalkboard. We were the lone survivors, and I felt lucky to have made it through with only a C grade to show for it.

Earlier during the semester there was the day some of the students decided to have a food fight in the cafeteria. I had nothing to do with the planning of this, only that my friends talked about it and had asked me if I'd join in. It was suppose to happen at exactly 5:10 p.m. that evening, right after they opened up for dinner. As cadets we had official midshipmen identification cards that allowed us into the cafeteria, which we entered just after the doors opened at 5:00 p.m. From there we received our meals at the buffet style serving area, and I sat with my friends at a long table, which was one of many being filled up with hungry cadets. As the clock on the wall ticked closer to ten minutes after five, everyone seemed to be waiting at the tables and not eating, which surprised me. Were there this many people really in on the food fight? Then at exactly 5:10 p.m.—we all looked around to see if anything would happen. When the first plate of food was tossed, it started a chain reaction of many plates being thrown, and then a lot more plates. Everyone was hit by some type of food, it seemed to be coming from all directions, and full plates splattered over many of us.

When everyone's ammo of food ran out, the plates suddenly stopped flying. There was a slight pause as people couldn't believe what'd just happened, and some cadets headed towards the front exit trying to escape. Quickly the oldest cadet in the bunch—he had gone through the U.S. Navy but entered as a fourth-class cadet—got there first to stop us. Mops were handed out and we all cleaned up the mess over the course of an hour. The staff in the cafeteria didn't even seem upset by this, almost as though they enjoyed it themselves. Nobody was reprimanded and it was all forgotten by everyone.

One of my friends in our 2-D division was sort of the leader of the group when it came to after-school activities. This usually involved drinking alcohol somewhere—often at one of the many bars in the area. Since we were all underage at this point, we'd go out and see if they'd serve us alcohol. Most times they did, and many times we had as many drinks as we wanted, but it was too easy to get into trouble doing these things. One of my friends was so drunk once that he put out his lit cigarette on top of a bar patron's head, and it almost caused a riot. I don't know how we got out of that one without any missing teeth.

There was even a bar at the end of the road right outside of the academy. We almost never went to it because it was so close to our campus, but on the last night before vacation everyone went out there to celebrate making it through another semester. The old guy who owned the place was serving us drinks and not carding anyone. He just seemed happy to have all of us in there at the same time, as every table was filled up with cadets.

I only had a few dollars left and bought a drink with my friends, and gave the owner a five dollar bill. He was taking all of our money anyways, so when he came back with the change, I asked if that was for the ten I'd given him. He looked surprised and left, then a minute later he came back extremely angry and threatened me saying there was no ten in the cash register. He started to yell how I was a liar (which I was). With all these cadets buying drinks, how could there not be a ten? What were the chances? My friends quickly came to my rescue saying how I didn't mean it, and it was all an innocent mistake. Eventually the owner gave in, but little did I know he'd go to the academy about it the next day.

I found out about this later after returning from vacation, when the head commandant was back from the cruise and inspecting me. We were all standing out by the flagpole at attention for inspection divided into our groups as always. Even though my uniform was spotless and my haircut was to regulation length, the commandant said my hair was too long and gave me twenty-five demerits. This was on the first day! I still hadn't put two and two together yet, so went and had my hair cut at the school barbershop by an old guy with a dozen tattoos on his arms. He claimed to be an ex-boxer and only talked about boxing the whole time he was cutting my hair. He ended up making it so short that not much was left, but at the next inspection the following day, the commandant gave me another twenty-five demerits. That meant I had fifty demerits and the semester was barely started! If I get twenty-five more during the next three months—they would kick me out of the academy.

Unfortunately, whenever a cadet received fifty demerits, they were always assigned special cleaning duties somewhere within the campus. However the commandant took me outside the main gate and showed me the sidewalk that led out to the bar at the end of the road. *So that's what this was all about!* He told me I was suppose to sweep and trim all the weeds and bushes along the sidewalk down the entire street, and clean the whole mess up to the end of the bar. Once that chore was finished, I was to tell him it was ready for inspection.

I guessed that since this was outside of our school grounds, he had no authority to make me clean any areas outside the campus, so I decided to skip trimming the weeds or sweeping any leaves. I did none of it. Lucky for me the commandant forgot all about it, at least I assumed he did. I never heard another thing about this from him, but the academy would get back at me later.

This was still the third semester of my first year, and since the training ship was back from the cruise, we had Shipboard Laboratory class again. There were also classes in Chemistry, Physics, English Composition and Business Statistics. Then there was the Survival Swimming class which was meant to teach us how to make it through a sinking ship alive.

The rest of the semester went by uneventfully; I minded myself and didn't get any more demerits. Eventually I made it all the way to the end until just before final exams, when one of my fellow classmates in 2-D told me he was failing with his grades. He told me how much he loved being at the academy and how much he wanted to eventually graduate. By this time I'd decided to improve my own grades from the first two semesters, having decided I was going to do my best and get my grades up to the highest level I could. This was due to my grade point average through the first two semesters averaging only a 2.70, which meant I was barely carrying a C+ average.

The cadet asking for my help mentioned he could definitely pass all of his classes except for one, and he begged for my assistance. He promised that if I gave him the answers to the final exam for that one class, he could pass the year and come back to study harder, and would never ask for my help again. I told him I'd have to think it over and get back to him.

I mulled it around during the day and eventually decided to help him, but told him it was only for that one class. It was also a one-time thing and after that, he was on his own, just as he'd promised me earlier. He happily agreed and I thought it wouldn't be such a big deal. After all, why should just one test stop someone from accomplishing what they really wanted in life?

During the following week, the final exam day arrived for our class. As everyone entered the classroom, we all picked out where to sit and I ended up seated in the row right in front of him. After the instructor handed out the tests, I went through it and concentrated on getting the best score I could. With about 20 minutes left I wrote down all the answers, but changed a few of them to be wrong on purpose, and then gave the list to the cadet I was helping. A couple of minutes later I looked back and was shocked to see him handing out the same answers to some of the other students! Oh well, there wasn't anything I could do about it—not without giving us all away.

After finals, I forgot all about this and left at the end of the semester to go home, assuming everything was fine and I'd easily passed my tests. Little did I know the class instructor had figured it all out, and they were ready for us when we returned from break the following semester.

At The Academy

Once back at the academy, the head commandant gave us our first morning inspection like always out by the flagpole. But during this he pointed some cadets out, including me, and afterwards had us go along with him to the administration building—where the dean of the school and our instructor were waiting inside of a large office to talk with us. We were informed that they knew all about the cheating on the final exam, and there had never been a cheating scandal in the history of the academy. We were all involved and they were going to determine the correct punishment for us; to be administered later. Then they let us leave.

The next day they served notice and started calling in cadets one by one to quiz us all on how everyone got the answers to the test. Since they'd all copied from the same answer list, it was easy enough to figure out who cheated. Eventually they got to me, and I sat down for my interview. The dean said they'd talked to all the other cadets caught cheating, and then asked me point blank if I gave them the answers to the test. My mind immediately raced to come up with an answer. I tried to figure out the possible punishments, the eventual outcome to certain answers, and how best to get away with this—all in what seemed like a split second.

And it quickly dawned on me what to do—I told him the complete truth. There was only one student who'd come to me about failing school, and if he didn't pass the test, he'd lose his chance to stay at the academy he loved. So I promised to only give him the answers to this one test, and only for this one class—I had no way of knowing he'd give them to those other fifteen cadets, and it was as shocking to me as it was to everyone else that he'd done it!

Then they told me to leave and said everybody would receive their decision from the investigative team very soon. Three days later they had us return to the administration building to hear the outcome, so we all assembled there anxiously. Incidentally, the one cadet who'd started all this hadn't returned for his second year, so he apparently failed even with my assistance (in other words, he must've lied about his grades). Then the final decision was given to us—all of the cadets who cheated had to take the whole class over again, and it was to be held at night. That was disappointing since on those evenings it meant no time for any after-school alcoholic refreshments. Most of those stuck were my closest friends at the academy, so I was rather surprised to see them caught doing this, I somehow always imagined them being smarter than that.

As for me, they said I didn't have to take the class over again, I wasn't given any demerits, and it was almost as if they did nothing to me. That was the most surprising thing of all. The one who created the scandal got no punishment, or perhaps they felt the one who'd asked me was responsible. Either way, I was happy with the outcome, but puzzled at the same time since it felt like I'd dodged another bullet.

To make room for the newest cadets, many of us now third-class midshipmen were picked to move into the lower dorm complex, which was much nicer and quieter than the old residence hall at the top of the stairs. These newer three-story buildings had larger rooms and more private showers for us to use. At one end they had the female cadets grouped together, and the rest were for the male cadets. This area was much more conducive to learning, as we had fewer steps to climb to reach our living quarters, and no slamming of doors in the middle of the night to contend with. Once we were assigned a room, we generally stayed in it until we either graduated or left the campus.

I was lucky as they assigned my room in this lower area along with my divisional friends, and we had the complex just above the barber and snack shops on the west end. This was a good place to stay and it had easy access to everything in the area, with about half as many stairs to climb as were needed to reach the upper areas of the campus.

After that close call with the cheating scandal, I mainly focused on staying out of trouble during the next semester. But it all started off crazy enough when I was aboard the training ship with a new cadet who'd just entered the academy. Our training ship, the Golden Bear, had tall masts both forward and aft, and for some reason during our watch the cadet decided to show me how well he could climb. He briefly disappeared from my sight and eventually yelled down to me. When I looked up and finally saw him, I couldn't believe he was at the very top of the forward mast-head. With no safety gear!

My mind imagined seeing him fall over fifty feet to the steel deck below and then splattering everywhere. I was instantly horri-fied. Quickly I yelled up for him to come down carefully, and after a long three minutes, I breathed a sigh of relief when he made it back down on deck. Amazingly, he acted all proud of himself for having climbed to the top. I mentioned how dangerous and stupid it was to do that without safety gear and before getting instruc-tions, since any of those rusty hand-holds could have broken free, or just a simple slip of his footing and I'd have been responsible. Fortunately for the both of us nothing had happened.

Meanwhile, the academy had allowed in new transfer students to fill in spots for the departing cadets who'd left or were dis-missed from the academy during the prior year. These transfer students were assigned to each division to round out the student body, and we got some new faces to go along with our returning 2-D members. I learned how it was smart of them to transfer in since they had avoided a whole year of cleaning, watch duties, and living in the noisy dorm building at the top of our campus, plus having to deal with a lot of fellow cadets who would drop out of school.

My grades for the prior semester had become much better, and they raised my GPA up to almost a 3.0 average. I'd even received a B in Physics from our math instructor, which was higher than he'd given me in Calculus. However, this next semester he was back to teach us Physics II, and I was told that he'd never given out an A to anyone in the history of the class. I had no way of knowing if it was true or not, but I decided to try and get one to see if it was even possible. So I studied hard for the first test and surprisingly got a 90% on it, then found out how everyone else did when he posted a summary of our grades outside of his office door. He would place a paper graph with a scale that went from 100 down to zero, and included a dot next to each spot that represented a cadet's score. For obvious privacy reasons he didn't include names along with them.

As the tests went along during the semester, he continued to post the test averages, so everyone could see where each of us stood compared to everyone else. I learned later that the actual scale itself was less important compared to where we were relative to each other. So someone below a seventy might still get a C despite that being under the theoretical scale—if many other students were also there. And as the semester progressed, I held my dot near the top of the page at the 90% level, which was an obvious A grade. Below me about ten points down was the nearest dot, under which the remainder were scattered in small groupings down into the lower sixties.

When we were almost half-way through the semester, something happened—one of the dots started to catch up to me by moving up the scale after each weekly test. Unfortunately, that's when I ended up having my one bad test, and it happened to be about optical lenses. It was a test where it showed a candle with its light passing through a couple of glass lenses containing certain characteristics, and we had to calculate what the candle looked like after its image left the final lens. And it was just before this test that I found out an amazing secret, but it was too late to help me out.

When I walked into my dorm room during lunch, I saw my room-mate looking over old tests and asked him what they were. He said our division had a file containing all of the old tests given out by the various instructors during their teaching years at the academy! He was busy learning off of this very lens test from the prior year, which had been graded and showed corrections by our whiz instructor.

I quickly studied it with only fifteen minutes left before I had to leave, but still did badly on the test. My low grade of sixty effectively dropped my class average enough under ninety percent so that I wasn't assured of an A anymore. At this point the other student who'd been racing up the scale with his dot passed me by and took over the top average for the class. There I was just under him, with the nearest trailing dots still another ten points grouped below us.

Thanks to having the old tests to study, it helped me to score a ninety on the final exam, yet it wasn't enough to raise my overall average enough and it still left me with an eighty-eight for the semester. On the last day he posted our final grades on his scale— he gave the top dot in the class an A, and gave my dot just below it an A-, which didn't actually exist as a grade. But being who he was, I guess he wanted to show everyone that I wasn't good enough to get an A, yet that's how they recorded it on my official transcript. I also did well enough with my other classes in Marine Transportation, Naval Architecture, Humanities and Naval Science to raise my overall average above a B for the first time. At least it was somewhat respectable now, and was much better than where I'd started out over a year earlier.

But next up for me and my fellow third-class cadets was our first cruise out to sea aboard our training ship. This was finally what we'd all really entered the academy to learn, and I wondered how it might be. Eventually, as my winter vacation dwindled away while at home, my anticipation and excitement for our cruise grew by comparison. *How would it be?* I packed up my belongings from the recommended list of items to take with us, and headed out. There was no looking back now!

2

It's Called Seasick

When I returned to the academy for the following winter semester, we took my first cruise aboard our training ship. The Golden Bear was 491 feet long with a beam (width) of 65 feet, and could steam along under ideal conditions at seventeen knots. She was originally built in 1940 for cargo and passenger trips between New Orleans and Buenos Aires, but was quickly taken into service by the U.S. Navy during World War II, and years later was transferred to the California Maritime Academy in 1971. I had scraped and painted enough of her steel decks up to this point to notice the signs left behind that she'd been used during the war. There were still remnants of circular rings on her decks that showed where they'd had the gun emplacements, and below decks was a magazine chute that led to the location where the ammo was stored.

The academy reminded us that these training voyages were intended to give us the appropriate sea time to sit for our third mate's license, and also to give us enough valuable experience to be a competent ship's officer when sailing after graduation. All of the time spent learning in the classroom was now meant to be applied during this training cruise. However, for the third-class cadets like myself who were taking their first cruise, we'd also end up being the ones to do all the dirty work aboard the ship. The technical term for this was ship's maintenance (in simple terms, we might write it down as mopping, painting, and scrubbing). Besides cleaning we'd also stand bridge watches and attend scheduled classes on seamanship, rules of the road, and communications. Meanwhile, the second-class cadets would move up and start using celestial navigation, while also directing us in our cleaning duties. Finally, the first-class cadets would concentrate on radar plotting, watch standing, rules of the road, and navigation.

Since we were still only unlicensed cadets, besides the captain on the ship, we also carried a licensed chief mate and second mate from the faculty staff, along with an outside third mate hired solely for this voyage. These mates were the ones legally standing their watches, but they had us cadets do as much as we could in the decision-making and navigation, while they still remained responsible for everything. The engineering cadets had the same situation as we did, but obviously were concerned with learning the engine room operations.

So after loading the training ship with all of our gear and supplies at the academy dock, we waved good-bye to our family members who'd come to see us depart, then we sailed out into San Francisco Bay and passed under the Golden Gate Bridge—on our way out to sea. Sailing aboard the training ship were 345 midshipmen, along with the necessary academy staff to complete a 9,000 mile voyage to ports in Long Beach, Cabo San Lucas, Tahiti, Hawaii, San Francisco and eventually ending up at our dock back in Vallejo.

Unfortunately, I hadn't been out on the ocean in quite some time, so had forgotten how rough it was on the West Coast in winter. Within an hour of leaving the San Francisco Sea Buoy behind, I was already feeling the effects, the constant swaying of the ship, the moving horizon as it went up and down as I stood still on deck. Even if I swayed against the ship to counter it, things still seemed to be disorienting. Slowly there was a raw sickness that took over my body, sort of like having the flu come on all at once. It even reminded me of being car sick with that feeling of impending death, or having a horrible hangover the next morning from a heavy drinking binge—and all I could do was try to fight it while holding out hope it might get better.

But after another two hours of this brooding sickness, it became a lost cause, and it happened over by the starboard railing when I finally gave in. This was after being served our first meal down in the mess which I'd barely eaten, then gone quickly back up on deck to get some badly needed fresh air. It was there when I noticed a strange smell coming from the forward part of the ship that made things worse. *Was someone else sick?* I'd hit that point where there was only one thing that could make me feel better, and with that thought, I glanced to both sides to check that no one was watching, then I lost what little dinner I'd eaten over the railing.

What a relief! I instantly felt much better after losing it, then waited a few minutes to make sure that's all I had, and went below to lay down in my bunk in the berthing area. I still had to stand the 8:00 to 12:00 watch that night, and that meant being on the bridge while switching between being the helmsman and a lookout. I even held out knowing I could've claimed sickness, but someone was going to stand the watch and I didn't want to start off on the wrong foot with my fellow cadets.

After getting in a short nap, I made my way up to the bridge for my watch, and at first I was the helmsman who steered the ship. It was my first try at the wheel. The Golden Bear actually had two steering wheels on the bridge, one was a large wooden wheel like you'd see on most old sailing ships, yet there was another smaller wheel that we normally used that had modern hydraulics which made steering easier. That's the one I used and it made the watch pass by faster—since I'd concentrate on steering instead of that returning feeling of impending seasickness.

In a back room behind the bridge, there was a course recorder that logged how well our helmsman was doing. It had a long needle that swung back and forth on a rolling sheet of paper to show the ship's course and all steering changes. So if a helmsman was doing a good job, we could see the course might vary by only a couple of degrees to either side, but if the helmsman was doing a bad job, it would display perhaps three to four degrees of swing to either side. Since this was my first turn at the wheel, when we checked my course recorder tape later, it was an example of how not to steer. At least for me there was nowhere to go but up.

Also, that night while on watch, I noticed how the bridge was one of the places where you really felt the rolling of the ship. That's because the higher one gets, the more you swing against the center of gravity of the vessel. So if you're feeling seasick, it's about the last place you want to be, as the constant rolling seems twice as worse. Eventually this wore on me as the night went along, to where I had to excuse myself and go to the head (a nautical term used at sea to mean the bathroom). Once I got the door closed—I threw up again, but fortunately it wasn't loud enough for the other cadets on the bridge to hear. Again, it made me feel better, and then I waited a minute before heading back out to the bridge for the rest of my watch. After making it through to the end, I had a decent night's sleep and was feeling better by the next morning as we headed south into calmer waters. Lucky me!

When we hit our next port in Long Beach, I went ashore and the first thing I bought was some Dramamine, which is a medication meant to stop motion sickness. Eventually I learned to always take a pill about an hour before leaving port if we stayed more than a couple of days inside the harbor, and it worked so well that I never became seasick again. It was interesting how after a couple of days out at sea, I'd get my "sea legs" back though, and was able to withstand anything, even the roughest of weather.

After leaving the next port, I learned of this funny gag that the upper class often played on the fresh cadets, and it was possible because the accumulated mail which the ship received would be passed out to everyone, so many of us could be seen on deck opening up our letters from home or elsewhere as we sailed out to sea. Someone would invariably ask where did everyone get the mail from, and the reply was always, "We picked it up at the mail buoy on the way out." Of course there wasn't a mail buoy, but they didn't know that. And since the answer sounded good, they always were tricked into believing it.

The cleanliness aboard ship was very important to the academy, and as third-class cadets we were the ones who handled the workload of mopping, sweeping and painting. Whenever we hit port or sat at anchor, some of us might be sent over the side to paint the rust stains along the hull. Since the ship was almost entirely coated with white paint, any stains on the outer surfaces looked worse than if she'd been painted with a darker color. To apply paint over the side we'd sit in something called a bosun's chair. It was attached to a line and placed where it was needed, then after we sat in it, they'd lower us to where the painting needed to be done. They'd also send along the paint can tied on a separate line, which was lowered nearby and then tied off. When there were a group of us cadets painting in the same area, we might have six or eight lines tied next to each other along the railings. Occasionally someone would accidentally untie the wrong line, and if it was the one holding up a cadet, they sometimes made a big splash when falling into the water below.

Around meals we were also given cleaning duties in the galley, such as washing the dishes and utensils for the entire crew that ate aboard three times a day. This was the one job I hated the most, especially using the food grinder where all of the leftover food was scraped from the plates. Once loaded up and turned on, it would grind the food and shoot it out over the side of the ship. Meanwhile, the galley also had to be mopped after each meal and everything wiped down as well—it was a lot of work cleaning up for the hundreds of people aboard. And who could forget that there was the laundry to do, as they'd also left that up to the third-class cadets to perform. It seemed like there were over a thousand pieces of clothing to do every day, seven days a week through the laundry room. It involved not only the washing and drying, but also the folding and placing of it on everyone's bunk.

Bathing on the ship consisted of salt-water showers, and while at first it was hard to get used to them, eventually I accepted it and never opened my eyes. I think the salt-water may have been good for my skin as I never had any outbreaks during the whole voyage. The only downside was that I couldn't get a lather up with the soap using salt-water, so it was harder to wash with. In the berthing area, each of us was assigned a locker to store our clothes, books and other items we'd brought aboard. These were located around the perimeter of the space, and bunk beds were positioned in long rows that stretched from one bulkhead to the other. Enough spots were left over that some hammocks were strung by cadets to sleep in as well. Since I was in 2-D, our berthing area was just forward of the galley. 1-D happened to be berthed as far forward as possible near the bow, and in rough seas I never understood how they ever got a wink of sleep. Even the stern area for 4-D wasn't as bad as the bow, since up forward you got the extra pounding of the waves against the hull, along with

22

the sudden jerking up and down as the bow beat into the swells. Perhaps they felt it was like being rocked to sleep in a baby's cradle, while having happy memories of their childhood every night.

The food that we were served is what you'd expect without having a 5-star chef aboard with us. It was very simple food, but we had different items on the menu during every day of the week. Some of it was quite good, but there was one item that was unfortunately served. In order to save money, they'd ordered chicken backs instead of chicken legs for the whole voyage. I'd never had chicken backs before, and I've never had them since. There was literally only two tiny pieces of meat to each chicken back—one on either side of the spine. So on the days when it was being served, everyone knew we'd end up hungry after dinner, plus all those chicken backs had to be ground up during cleaning duties. They generally used the same menus over again on a rotating basis, so we had chicken backs and hunger once a week for the whole voyage, at least until they finally ran out of them.

Whenever we approached or left a port, the ship would have a bow lookout up forward, and I happened to be assigned this as we entered Cabo San Lucas. After we turned around the point to sail in, suddenly I spotted a group of whales in the calm seas ahead, and they seemed to be crossing in front of the ship on almost a collision course. I didn't know if these should be reported to the bridge, but I imagined us hitting one and a large part of the forward hull being ripped open on impact. Quickly I called the bridge on the radio plugged into the communications port, and warned them about whales dead ahead. They may have laughed about it, but had I not reported them and something happened, they certainly would've blamed me.

After making it into port, we anchored just off the entrance, which meant taking launches from the training ship to get ashore. Those launches had been loaded on the forward hatch earlier while still at the academy, and now they were lowered over the side to be used in port. After getting them into the water, this was a slow process since each launch only carried a dozen people—and there were hundreds wanting to get ashore as fast as possible. The first night a few of the cadets were allowed to go ashore early by launch, with the bulk of us to go ashore the next day. One of the cadets that made it out went to a pharmacy and tried to buy some Valium, which the pharmacists reported to the Mexican police. He spent the night in jail as a result, and the next morning they had me go ashore with the rescue party, since I was the only one aboard who spoke fluent Spanish. When we made it out to the police headquarters and they saw us in our white uniforms with CMA hats, I didn't have to say much. All I told them was we were here to get our cadet back, and they released him to us without a word. This was done first thing in the morning, so I got to be one of the first cadets ashore and had a few extra hours of liberty as a result.

Later that day, after the others in 2-D joined me ashore, most of us went swimming at the beach out by the point. Since it was at the very tip of Baja California, we were located where two oceans were converging and it made for some rough waves at times. We even tried body-surfing, but found out that they were far too strong to ride in the middle of winter. I got rolled by one wave and felt lucky to come out of it in one piece.

In my division I'd become friends with everyone in my class, and surprisingly there was one who admitted he'd never drank much alcohol in his life, at least he mentioned it with a straight face. Just by chance after returning to the ship we were talking about it, and he asked me to hang out with him the following day, which I assumed meant to go out drinking. So the following day after making it ashore on a launch, we ended up at the bar over-looking the point of Cabo San Lucas just before dusk. I told the bartender what we wanted, and quickly he lined up shots of tequila for us both, along with some mescal with the worm in the glass. After we finished a few shots, my friend declared he loved the stuff, so we kept drinking over a couple of hours until it became pitch dark outside, and by then we were really feeling the effects of the shots. It was getting late by then so we left the bar and headed down the hill to go back to the training ship.

We made it to the dock below and boarded the waiting launch, which had a cadet at the controls, but on the way out to the ship my friend started to act funny. He went from being a nice guy to becoming mean for some reason, and it wasn't something I'd expected. Once we got aboard the training ship, he started to pick fights with other cadets in our berthing area, including threatening one of the first-class cadets who came in to quiet him down. That was the one that really got him into trouble, and the next day along with his hangover, he found out his conduct was being reviewed by the head commandant. He'd determine an appropriate punishment later, which left my friend wondering what was to come next. Eventually the decision of demerits and loss of liberty was explained at the next Captain's Mast, and that turned out to be the last time my friend ever went drinking ashore with me.

After departing the anchorage at Cabo San Lucas, we watched it fade off into the distance while steering a new course for the small island of Tahiti. This area is well known, and was made famous due to a mutiny aboard the H.M.S. Bounty in 1789—where Captain Bligh was set adrift after Fletcher Christian took over the ship. The location of the island was also important to us because it meant we'd be crossing the equator on the trip down, and there's an old tradition at sea for those who've never done that before. Sailors who haven't crossed it are referred to as pollywogs, but once the appropriate tests are passed along with a crossing, then they turn into shellbacks.

During the trip down, we hit the expected doldrums along the way, which meant no wind seemed to blow for days on end. While the sea life we saw during this stretch of ocean covered everything you'd expect, it also included something strange. At night as we got further along into warmer waters, we noticed tiny sea creatures that glowed in the ocean. It only happened when they became disturbed in the wake of the ship, and since the bow was constantly hitting waves while creating wash-water, the creatures would put on a spectacular glow at night. Sometimes it was much brighter than at other times, but it was beautiful to be sailing through the ocean with a glowing trail of wake along both sides of the ship along the way.

Then the excitement grew as we neared the equator, until finally all the shellbacks aboard prepared the appropriate tests for us pollywogs. These were set up on the forward deck, with the first test having a "doctor" and a "nurse" cadet give us a physical to make sure we were fit enough to proceed—then they'd squirt some tobacco sauce into our mouths and see how well our reflexes were. A second test was with the largest cadet who had the biggest belly, he'd put Crisco all over himself and we had to rub our faces on him. The more we rubbed, the harder it was to see. Then we went to the next test, which was having someone discharge a CO_2 fire extinguisher all over us, making our skin very cold to the touch.

But the worst test of all came last—they'd filled an inflated life raft with dirty water and food scraps from the galley, including everything else to make it as filthy as possible to swim through. Some shellbacks were stationed with buckets on both sides to douse us whenever we lifted our heads up for air. Unfortunately, someone had swallowed some of the dirty water before and had vomited in the mix as well. That made it ten times worse when my turn came. They'd even stretched a large net over the whole raft so we had to swim under it, but we all made it through the tests and became proud shellbacks, and we were issued official cards from the captain to prove it.

Imperium Neptuni Regis

Know ye that Mark H. Glissmeyer on this 13th day of February, 1983, crossed the equator at Longitude 134 degrees West. Thus he may be respected as one of our trusty shellbacks.

Signed by:

Davey Jones—His Royal Scribe

Neptunus Rex—Ruler of the Raging Main

After making the equator crossing, we continued on to Tahiti, where we tied up along a pier that extended out from the main harbor at Papeete. This was in a beautiful area of the island, and immediately after we got there some local vendors set up across the way to sell us things, which some cadets couldn't resist buying. One vendor in particular was selling little pieces of meat on skewers, and they must have tasted good as some cadets were seen eating them once we were allowed ashore. Believe it or not, we were later told this was dog meat being sold to us, as it was an old Tahitian custom, which was considered a delicacy and prized food by the locals.

The nearby island of Moorea was a wonderful trip to take, it had even more things to do and many of the cadets took the trip over. While the island of Tahiti wasn't quite the paradise it was portrayed in the movies, with topless women everywhere and drunken parties every night, we all had fun and enjoyed our stay. Some of the guys in my division had even rented a car and rolled it on a mountainside road, leaving me glad I'd missed out on their adventure. But when we departed Tahiti, everyone was relaxed and happy, even though a long voyage lay ahead on the way to Hawaii.

After departing Papeete, we headed north and crossed over the equator for the second time, where the captain decided to stop the ship so we could do some painting aloft. After a half-hour of sitting idle, some sharks suddenly showed up to see what the big white ship was doing out in the middle of nowhere. Actually, I was thinking the same thing about the sharks. What were they doing here when there wasn't anything around for hundreds of miles? A couple of them were very large, and one in particular seemed to be almost thirty feet long. That one swam like it owned the ocean, with the other sharks staying out of its way. One thing was sure, none of us were going to swing in a bosun's chair over the side with that thirty foot shark swimming underneath us. That quickly ended our hull painting plans for the day.

As we continued on and got closer to Hawaii, the dolphins showed up again, and loved to follow the ship whenever we got near them, almost as if they'd been reunited with an old friend. They'd jump all along the hull, and if close to the bow, would swim and jump across it. There was a dolphin among them that was quite good at it, and its picture was taken by many cadets. Eventually though they'd become tired and lose interest, leaving us to continue on our way without them.

These long stretches of the voyage were also useful for completing our required classes for the cruise. Besides being graduation requirements, they gave us important experience in the tasks needed for sailing at sea, such as with seamanship. We had wire splicing to learn, where we used a marlinspike and a vise to form an eye at the end of a wire cable. This wasn't an easy task to accomplish, but we all got the hang of it eventually. We also learned how to tie various knots, some of which we used all the time—like a bowline or a monkey's fist. Other knots we learned were the sheepshank, clove hitch, rolling hitch and Turk's head, to name a few. We got tested on all the knots, including how to make a small bag using canvas—which is called a ditty bag.

The monkey's fists made in seamanship class were large coiled knots placed at the end of a messenger line, and were used as a weight when throwing them to the longshoremen when docking in port. Since you couldn't just toss a regular mooring line due to its heavy weight, you first needed a lighter line that they could catch. Throwing the monkey's fist was always some free entertainment for us. Usually there was someone who threw one and came up short, so it splashed in the water before reaching the dock. Cadets would then laugh as the line had to be coiled back up all wet and tossed again for a second try.

When we finally reached the big island of Hawaii, we docked in Hilo and used our newly made monkey's fists to help get the ship tied up. None of us had ever been to Hawaii before, so once we got shore leave, we rented a car and went on a tour of the island. The large Kilauea volcano had started erupting in January, so they had that area of the island closed off to visitors. Instead, we drove out past where they had large grazing areas for cattle on the eastern side, and then to the North Shore area where the surfers were concentrated. The police were even nice to us when we got pulled over for speeding, and let us off with just a warning.

After we left the big island, we briefly stopped at Maui for a day and had a party on the beach. Then we sailed for the last stretch of our voyage on the way over to San Francisco. This was where we wrapped up anything we needed to finish before the cruise ended, and everyone looked forward to finally getting back home. From the lovely blue waters we'd been sailing in, the ocean slowly turned more greenish over time, until we finally viewed the California coastline and the Golden Gate Bridge—a sign we were nearly there. At the San Francisco Sea Buoy we were met by the pilot boat, with many cadets watching as the pilot jumped onto the pilot ladder and came aboard.

We conveniently docked by the downtown section of San Francisco near Fisherman's Wharf. Off in the distance was the famous Alcatraz Island, a place I was looking forward to taking a tour of. When we finally got shore leave, five of us went out to Chinatown to eat at a nice restaurant, and one of them looked promising, so we went inside. By the time we were served, the portions of food were so small it would take a hundred dollar bill just to get a decent meal between us. I wondered how all these locals could afford this place? We paid for what we ate and left, then found a more affordable restaurant up the street.

After departing San Francisco, we sailed the short distance through the North Bay and arrived back at the California Maritime Academy, where we tied up to finish off our cruise. *What a relief!* I'd probably folded over two thousand pieces of clothing during the voyage, used fifty gallons of white paint on all surfaces of the ship, including myself, passed the seamanship, watch standing, and communication requirements—and had returned back to the academy safely. That was the toughest test we had, and it meant I'd no longer be a junior cadet again. I had made it!

3

A Second Time

When I returned back to the academy after having enjoyed my spring break, there was a new feeling of how different things were. Everything felt and looked even better, now having the stress of one cruise finally under my belt. There was also the nice feeling of knowing that my time at the academy was almost half over, since finishing this current semester would mark the start of becoming a second-class cadet.

Yes, there were still a few general education classes left to take, but the nautical curriculum was getting more focused, with required classes consisting of Ship's Stability, Radar Piloting and Seamanship. I also had to take one advanced writing class though, and it was for a letter grade this time. One of our classes even got a new instructor who came across from the U.S. Merchant Marine Academy, however some of the students warned me that he expected our shoes to be shined prior to attending class, and was reprimanding those who failed to follow orders.

I decided to heed those warnings by going to my dorm room and putting on a nice shine to see what he said. And sure enough, after we entered his class that afternoon, he looked over all of our shoes. He walked down each aisle of cadets looking down with a scorned face at their dirty shoes, until he came to my desk and had a surprised look. Not only were my shoes acceptable, he even mentioned how impressed he was with their shine. But for our academy, it seemed he was coming on as too strict, for this was to be the only semester he would teach us before leaving, either out of his own choice or through the academy dismissing him.

For our after-school activities, our excursions now included friendly trips to the nearby city of Fairfield for games of racquet-ball. We would drive out to play there at least once a week, and one of my friends often joked inside the nearby gas station that we were mental patients visiting from the nearby hospital. Sadly they seemed to believe him, at least they pretended to. It must have been more of a reflection on him than the rest of us though. How crazy can someone act when filling up a gas tank?

On one such racquetball trip, my car got rear-ended by a truck pulling a heavy boat, and it got a good whack on the back hood. My father received a substantial amount of money from the insurance company for the dent, and both myself and my friend got pain and suffering money for our experience. Apparently insurance companies would rather pay a small amount up front for total immunity from an accident. All they did was tape me over the phone saying I'd never prosecute them for any physical harm due to the driver's negligence, and the insurance check arrived in the mail.

Occasionally we were still going out to the nearby bars on weeknights, and later during the semester we came back late after another trip out. Once I'd parked my car in the upper parking lot at the academy, we made it down the long flight of stars and I challenged my friend to a wrestling match on the front lawn of the administration building. He agreed, and so we locked arms and began trying to knock each other over using brute strength, but quickly we both got very tired. At that point I congratulated my friend, and we laid down flat on the grass to rest. That's when everything started to turn blurry. All those drinks that we'd had earlier plus the wrestling didn't mix well together, so I fell into a deep dream while resting. Time flew by after all that whiskey, until I imagined hearing some words coming from somewhere.

"Hey... Hey, you."

It was very weak sounding and seemed very far away. Then after a minute, it happened again.

"Hey... Hey, wake up."

I still imagined that I was dreaming this, at least I had to be. But when the sound of a jeep arrived and a very strong voice shouted, I woke up and realized who it was.

"Hey, why are you sleeping on the administration grass in front of the entrance? They'll be opening up in fifteen minutes, you'd better get out of here!"

It was the cadet on watch driving the old jeep who'd woken us up, and my friend looked around as puzzled as I was. We were still lying on the grass after wrestling the night before, and must have been blitzed to stay sleeping all night. Fortunately this guy on watch happened by in the morning and awoke us before the faculty staff started arriving in a few minutes. We quickly got up and went off to prepare for our classes before anyone else found out about it.

Since learning about the secret file we had with the old class tests, I'd been using them all semester to help raise my test scores. Eventually we made finals week, and again I scored well on my tests. Of course I wouldn't know how well until the results were mailed to me during my summer break, but later to my surprise, I received all A's except for one B—which ended up being my best semester. It was hard to beat that one, and it raised my average up to a 3.24, which I'd maintain throughout the rest of my time at the academy.

After my summer break ended, it was time to return and start my fall schedule of classes. Since a new group of cadets were arriving to replace those graduating, that meant I was bumped up to a second-class cadet. It showed on the curriculum and my semester schedule, since there was a Leadership class, Navigation Lab, Rules of the Road, Ship's Operations, and Ship's Medicine. It was rounded out with Transportation Management and Advanced Composition (again).

Some of the instructors were around for only a few classes, so when it came time to start my Ship's Medicine class, the instructor behaved like someone who'd been here and done that. At first he sat down on a stool and told us all about himself. Then after a while he took out some index cards and handed them to the closest cadet seated nearby. Even though the instructor already had our names on the official class list, he asked each of us to write down our names—last name first, first name last—on an index card and return them to the end of the row, where he'd collect them all. I wondered why he didn't just write the names down on all the cards himself?

When the blank cards came by me, I took two cards and passed the rest on to the next cadet seated to my right. On one card I wrote my real name—last name first, first name last. On the other card, I took out a different pen and wrote a fake name—last name first, first name last. I carefully looked around to be sure no one saw me doing this, and when it came time to hand them back in, the guy next to me gave me the stack and I added the card with my real name on top, and added the fake name to the bottom. I then passed them to go down the line to the next cadets, and then back to the instructor.

Since this was only a once-a-week class, I left after it ended and didn't think much about it for the remainder of the week. An interesting thing though occurred when my economics teacher asked me to come into his office, where he told me about a tutoring lab he wanted to start. It was to run from 7:00 p.m. to 8:30 p.m. every Monday, Tuesday and Wednesday night. He said I was the first student he was approaching to become a tutor, and asked me if I wanted the job. Without hesitation, I told him it would be my honor to do it. He mentioned that I'd be paid the California minimum wage to start, and happily I thanked him for the opportunity. He also asked one of my friends to become a tutor along with me, so the two of us were scheduled to open up the tutoring lab and help anyone starting the following week.

The excitement of this tutoring job made me forget all about my Ship's Medicine class. Eventually when we had that class the following week, the same instructor sat on a stool and started to read off the names from the index cards we'd all handed in earlier. I wasn't paying much attention, but as each last name was called out from a card, a cadet in the class would answer back to him by saying, "Here!" When the instructor was about half-way through calling out our names, he came to the fake one I'd placed in the pile.

"Meoff."

No cadet answered him back.

"Meoff, are you here?"

No one answered him again.

"Does anyone know where Meoff is?"

Finally another cadet in the classroom who was often a jokester asked the instructor, "Is that Jack you're looking for?"

The face on the instructor said it all, he quickly said, "Oh crap!" and immediately all the cadets starting laughing out loud as the instructor's face turned beet red with embarrassment. He then threw the fake card into the trashcan nearby, and sat there for a moment while everyone continued laughing. It was amazing how another cadet had guessed the fake name like that.

While I couldn't believe how perfect that joke had gone, it made me feel bad for having pulled it on the instructor—I thought he would catch the fake name before ever reading it aloud. Luckily I was careful enough so he couldn't trace it back to me. Had he found out, it probably would've ended my days at the academy, but I knew that risk going in. And I was careful to never tell any of the other cadets it was me afterwards, the last thing I wanted was everyone knowing the new school tutor had made a fool out of an instructor. It was also to be the last prank I played on anyone like that again. With three of my weeknights now occupied helping others, I wasn't out drinking with my friends much anymore. The rest of the semester went well, and after I received my grades during winter break, it was time to prepare myself mentally for our upcoming cruise.

After everyone arrived back at the academy from vacation, we loaded all the supplies and equipment needed for our next voyage before waving good-bye to our family and friends on the dock, then we departed Vallejo in January of 1984 aboard the Golden Bear. We were scheduled for stops in various ports along the West Coast including Vancouver, Portland, Long Beach, Zihuatanejo, Puerto Vallarta, and Panama. And when we hit the same heavy swells outside the Golden Gate Bridge like on the earlier trip the year before, there was no seasickness for me this time. I'd taken some Dramamine before departing from the dock, and it worked perfectly like a charm. Once we passed the San Francisco Sea

Buoy, we headed south and made our way down towards Mexico, which was scheduled to be the first leg of our southern trip.

Since I was now a second-class midshipman, there wasn't going to be any of the cleaning aboard the training ship like I'd done on the last cruise. No more chipping, painting and scrubbing, no more doing the laundry, washing dishes, and emptying the garbage pails. This trip was meant to focus on supervision of the third-class cadets, along with watch standing and celestial navigation. I also was to learn how my friends had matured and wanted more adult entertainment when going ashore, and that happened when we finally docked at our first port.

This was a stop in the Mexican city of Zihuatanejo, and if that resort wasn't enough, there was a side trip possible to the nearby town of Ixtapa as well. Once we received our shore leave that afternoon, my friends decided we all should go out for some drinks away from town, but there was a catch this time—it was to be a trip out to the red zone. As we all learned soon enough, the taxicab drivers in Mexico could take us to find anything we wanted, so once we piled into the first taxi we found, all I had to say were those two magic words in Spanish to the driver, "Zona roja."

The taxi driver stepped on the gas and took the five of us away, where we headed out into the jungle roads away from the training ship. We wound around to the south for a bit and eventually parked outside a secluded bar in a dirt parking lot. As we all entered inside, the taxi driver followed behind us and took a seat by the front entrance. We went in further and sat down at the large table in the center of the room, where we ordered drinks from the bartender. On the side wall I noticed a long line of closed doors that probably went into smaller bedrooms, but that was only a guess.

The prostitutes inside were seated together along the front of the bar, and quickly came over to talk with us after we'd finished ordering. Since none of my friends spoke Spanish, and none of the whores spoke enough English, everyone knew it wasn't going to be very lengthy. It also didn't take words to notice this was a very motley group of older prostitutes we had to choose from. I told them in Spanish to let us have a couple of drinks and we'd eventually decide, since none of us were in a hurry. After we finished our first drinks and talked things over, we ordered another round from the bartender, and then another round after that one. The strange thing was the prostitutes looked worse the more I drank, not better. However, I knew one of my friends who came with us was still a virgin, so I picked one out and told her in Spanish that my friend wanted to be with her—and asked her how much. She had a big gold tooth in front and looked pretty worn, but my friend had a few drinks in him already so she probably looked OK at this point.

When I asked him, my friend said yes, so we gave her the money and the two of them went through one of the side doors nearest to us. Then about ten minutes later, my friend popped his naked torso out the door while holding a blanket around his waist, and said to me she wanted more money. I told him to nod yes to her, everything's OK—after which he shut the door again. Another ten minutes later they came out together, but she surprisingly never asked for the extra money. And after we got back to the ship, my friend was happy for weeks, but it's a good thing he wasn't sober enough to see what he'd slept with.

After we departed Zihuatanejo, we sailed south and I got into the routine of attending classes, supervising the third-class, standing watches, and also doing celestial navigation. Since celestial navigation has such a long history, I won't repeat it here, but it's what seafarers have used to navigate on ocean voyages since before Christopher Columbus. It was always the one thing available when the weather cooperated, but if the weather turned rotten, a navigator had to rely on past fixes for their estimated position.

Aboard our training ship we attended classes at sea to get us up to speed on the proper way to shoot stars twice a day with a sextant—at dawn and at dusk. Now I wouldn't know it at the time, but later when I started working aboard commercial ships, we never used celestial navigation. We relied on getting satellite fixes alone when out at sea, as all one had to do was read the ship's position off the computer screen and plot it on a chart. That was much simpler and easier than squinting at stars through a sextant.

But I didn't know that at the time, and it didn't really matter. The academy was all about preparing us for the U.S. Coast Guard exams for our license, and the U.S. Coast Guard tested everyone applying for a deck license on this subject, so it had to be taught. It was also an integral part of what every navigator needed to know, for if one didn't understand the basics of celestial navigation, they'd really be missing out on its core foundation. And since the academy was all about preparation, as far as I know everyone in their history had passed all the exams and went on to obtain their licenses, so they had a one hundred percent success rate going in with us.

One other interesting thing necessary for our license was we needed to become proficient at using the Morse code. This may sound simple enough, but we were to learn how to read the letters as they were flashed to us using a small blinking light, and it took a lot of practice to accomplish it. While most of the letters were easy to remember, such as one dot being the letter E, two dots being the letter I, and one dash being the letter T, by the time we included all the letters of the alphabet out to X, Y and Z, they became quite complicated. Patience was needed since between letters there was a slight pause, this was so we'd catch where one letter ended and the next one started. Then we had to write things down on our test paper without looking away from the flashing light, or else we might miss a dash or a dot. Eventually everyone figured out how to do this, and we practiced until everyone got it right.

We also had the Rules Of The Road book to learn, and this was gone over until it was memorized from the front cover to the last page. Just as there are rules when driving a car on land, there are rules that apply to ships at sea. The book explained when certain vessels have a right-of-way over other vessels in various circumstances. For example, a sailing vessel has the right of way over a power-driven vessel, but a fishing vessel has the right-of-way over a sailing vessel. Even a seaplane on the water has to follow the rules. The book has rules for overtaking other vessels, when vessels are crossing one another, or when having a head-on situation. Then there were sections on carrying lights and day shapes. We also had to memorize the sound and light signals being used at sea depending on the circumstances. The more we studied these rules, the more confusing they seemed to become.

On this leg of the cruise I was surprised when the Southern Cross suddenly appeared at night, not knowing it was visible from such northerly latitudes. Once we passed Costa Rica, we eventually made it to Panama City, which turned out to be another interesting port after we'd docked and gone ashore. Outside the harbor we could see all the ships anchored as they waited their turn to enter the Panama Canal, which was close by across the breakwater. The academy had arranged for those interested to go see the Miraflores locks, where the ships moved along as they passed through the canal. I took this opportunity to tour the visitor's center and museum they had which explained the construction and operation of the locks, along with the history of the Panama Canal itself. Afterwards we headed back to the city, where I joined my friends to take in some local sightseeing.

We left and walked up the main street for a while until one of my friends saw the flashy casino up ahead, telling us he wanted to go in and try the slot machines. I hadn't brought much money with to waste on betting, but my other friends insisted on trying the casino, so I reluctantly agreed to go along. Inside the place were long rows of slot machines everywhere, yet the place was eerily empty. There wasn't a single gambler at any of the machines I saw—not even one. That should have been a red flag for us to turn around and walk out, instead my friend told me the best way to win was to put dollar coins into the machines displaying the biggest payout. Twenty dollars for him and ten for me went in, yet nothing came back out in winnings. My other friends had the same bad luck; every coin they put in was taken by the one-armed bandits. We lost everything we'd bet and left feeling like idiots, realizing that the casino was nothing more than a tourist trap for suckers.

From there we walked further up the main street until we came to an intersection where we could go one of three ways. My friend told us to try this way, so we started walking in that direction. A couple of old Panamanian women were walking towards us and shook their fingers at us. Then they used their hands to show themselves slitting their throats. We stopped immediately and thanked them, then turned around and wisely went back to the ship.

On our last day in Panama City, we found a local taxi and asked the driver if the city had a red zone nearby. He laughed and told us to get in, then took us on a short drive to someplace within the city limits. When he parked it seemed much nicer than the place we'd visited near Zihuatanejo, and after entering the front doors, we sat at a large table to the side of the bar. Even the prostitutes here were much younger and prettier, and one in particular I found very attractive. After we ordered and got our drinks, a small group of them came over to our table to see what we wanted. I told the small one in Spanish that we should leave together after I was finished with my drink.

A couple of minutes passed by and I reminded her, but quickly guzzled down the rest of my beer after she looked back at me with an impatient stare like time is money. So then we left together, and she took me back into a room past the long nearby corridor. I paid the price for her services, and she briefly left the room—then she came back a moment later and turned down the lights. The time went by very quickly after undressing, until what seemed like only five minutes later there came a loud knock on the door. *Nope, not even finished yet.* What the hell? What else could I think? But luckily she was a pro and I ended up being happy more than once, that knock must have only been a warning.

After we dressed and arrived back at the bar, I was surprised to see all my friends still there at the same table drinking. These were probably the best whores we could find in a hundred miles, yet none of them wanted any? I was happy though, so it didn't matter to me—it had made my trip to Panama. After finishing one more drink, we left to head back to the ship, taking the same taxi that had brought us out to begin with.

Once we departed Panama aboard the training ship, we steered north this time, on a course headed up the West Coast towards

Mexico again—and that meant doing more celestial navigation. We were getting better at timing things now, and had the routine down of when to expect our next readings. When we prepared to take them before dusk, we'd use a wheel that had the direction and heights of the stars at certain times, and we'd set it for our observation time. We always tried to pick out the three brightest stars that were 120 degrees apart along the horizon. Those would be the ones to give us the best possible fix on our ship's position. Once we got ready, we took our sextant, a wristwatch, and the star wheel up on deck to one of the gyro repeaters that showed the compass card with the ship's heading. So if a star was going to appear bearing ninety degrees with an altitude of forty-seven degrees above the horizon, we'd set our sextant to forty-seven degrees and wait for it to appear bearing ninety degrees according to the compass card.

Then after the Sun went down and the night sky slowly turned to dusk, we had to worry about something else. Since not only does the sky turn dark—so does the horizon, which was needed to shoot the altitude of the stars. When using a sextant, the reflection of a star is brought down to the horizon and then swung from side-to-side until we got an exact height, then we'd quickly note the time of the sighting along with its height measurement. We did that for three stars before losing the horizon, and then went down below to determine our ship's position by performing the necessary calculations.

And there were a whole lot of those calculations to do—from the reading of the stars, to adjusting them to the correct time, and then to the star heights, and how they plotted on a graph. Sometimes if I did a really good sighting where all of the stars lined up perfectly, there would only be a small dot where the lines of position for each sighting met together. At other times I could end up with a large triangle instead, and have to use the center of that for our ship's position. These were handed in and graded on how accurate the sightings were.

Besides shooting the available stars with a sextant, we were also taught how to use the Sun and the Moon to help determine our ship's position. The Sun was available to shoot whenever it was visible above the horizon, and the Moon could be used for the same purpose. But it was always harder for me to get an accurate reading on the Moon using a sextant—since it moved so quickly across the sky. For every four seconds I was off in timing the sighting, I'd be nearly a nautical mile off in longitude once it was plotted. And since I was only using a regular wristwatch to time my sightings, it would have to be checked against the official ship's chronometer. Usually a correction was needed between the two, yet the chronometer had a correction of its own to get to true time. It was confusing enough that four seconds was easy to miss by, and if any corrections were done improperly, it probably meant being off by many more seconds. But eventually we figured it out through practice, repetition and testing. And that meant doing sextant readings twice a day while the weather cooperated with us at sea.

After we continued sailing far enough up the coast, the next port we stopped at was Puerto Vallarta. The entire resort became visible thanks to the calm seas and perfect weather, but upon arriving, I couldn't believe what else was out there. Thousands of sea snakes were on top of the ocean resting together, just hanging out for some reason. It was quite scary to see them everywhere, with horrible thoughts of someone falling into the water and being bitten by them. Even scarier was that they weren't very far off from the beach—where all the tourists could be seen walking around.

It reminded me of when I was an exchange student living with a poor family in Mexico, and had attended the same school as the other poor Mexicans, in what turned out to be the hottest summer of my life. There was no air conditioning anywhere, and opening a window on their house meant inviting dozens of mosquitoes in to bite us. I'd lay in bed at night and sweat until I was finally too tired to stay awake anymore. Sometimes during the day I'd go out snorkeling in the ocean to cool off, and that was when I saw a sea snake flipping over rocks with its head. But that was only one sea snake, compared to the thousands swimming here.

Needless to say, I didn't go swimming in the ocean during our stay in Puerto Vallarta, and instead preferred a relaxing shore leave for a couple of days. Then we sailed for our next port farther north, heading up towards California. During this time our celestial navigation class had added one of the easier things for us to learn—how to determine a ship's latitude. This was actually quite easy to do, as we could use either the Sun or the North Star to do it.

We first were taught how a sextant was used to come up with our noon latitude. This was done by observing the Sun, and knowing that it arcs higher into the sky throughout the morning, yet once it passes noon, the Sun starts to decline in the sky. While using a sextant we'd get the highest reading that the Sun made above the horizon, and plot that as a line of position. By using the time that it occurred, we'd also get us our ship's latitude at that exact moment. By contrast, the hard part of navigation was always getting the ship's longitude correct. In order to get that, it required a very accurate timepiece aboard the ship, and until they'd developed an accurate chronometer, it had always eluded the early navigators.

The North Star was also used to determine our latitude, where its height above the horizon ended up being fairly close to that of our ship's position. If we shot the North Star and it happened to be at thirty-eight degrees in altitude, we'd make some corrections to the reading, but it would give us a final latitude somewhere close to that. Of course, the North Star could be shot at both dawn and dusk, and if we added in a noon sighting using the Sun, we could check our ship's latitude up to three times a day.

On entering the Port of Long Beach, my money was running low enough so that I wouldn't be drinking with my friends here, instead preferring to take a tour of the Queen Mary that was moored nearby—her being the famous ocean liner used for Atlantic passenger services prior to World War II. But to our surprise along the way, we went in and had a bite to eat at a diner that had waitresses all wearing only lingerie. I ordered a cheese sandwich, but the place was really only meant for looking, not good eating. From the window seats we spotted the geodesic dome housing the Spruce Goose, once flown by the billionaire Howard Hughes.

A Second Time

After departing Long Beach, an afternoon was spent over by Catalina Island conducting anchoring drills. The charted waters on the east side of the island showed they fall off rapidly, allowing us to successfully anchor multiple times, yet one attempt happened before the ship was close enough to the shoreline. That meant the weight of the anchor and its chain were all placed on the brake pad built into the windlass. The chain kept running out until it was finally stopped before reaching the end—showing how weak the built-in brake was. Everyone learned a lot about anchoring either way, and it turned into a good learning experience for all involved.

The third-class cadets had so far been behaving themselves while doing their cleaning duties under our supervision. We made sure they were washing the laundry, sweeping up the passageways, folding every piece of clothing, and placing it all on the appropriate bunks. There was the mess area to clean up as well, including washing the dishes, sweeping and mopping the deck, and using the garbage disposal to eliminate the leftover food. Then there was the painting to be done everywhere—to the ship's hull, the bulkheads, the overheads, and to the railings. Everything was first chipped and wire brushed to get rid of any rust spots, then a coating of red lead was painted on to seal the bare metal, and finally a finishing coat was painted everywhere. By the end of the trip we saw work-clothes covered with many splotches of paint in a sort of camouflage pattern—something proudly to be worn as a sign of accomplishment.

But with all of this training and supervision came the resulting lack of privacy, especially on a training ship that carried hundreds of people aboard. There was one place aboard, though, where we could get total privacy that wasn't commonly known, and that was in the ship's lifeboats. They even had a nickname—being called the love boats. Ships were required to carry enough lifeboats to take an entire crew safely away from a ship ever since legislation was passed after the RMS Titanic sank in 1912. Our lifeboats were rated at a capacity of seventy persons each, so they were roomy enough to use for sleeping or to read a book in when they weren't covered (and they could be used for other things too).

The Golden Bear was originally built mostly as a cargo ship, with masts and booms using winches to run pallets in and out from her cargo holds. And in all my time working on the training ship, that included being out at sea and also ashore at the academy, I never recall anyone getting seriously injured. That was pretty impressive when you consider there were dangers lurking around every bulkhead during all the projects we worked on. From being hoisted high up for chipping and painting, to doing cargo operations using the winches and cargo booms, to having heavy pallets swung around and being lowered, or when moving lifeboats around and launching them over the side. We completed lots of dangerous tasks, but never had any accidents. I only wish that safety record would follow with me to when I worked aboard commercial ships later, but that wasn't to be the case. It's ironic, but after our next stop in Portland, that's where we lost our anchor on the way out, having to sail up to British Columbia with only a single anchor left aboard (but no injuries). Fortunately we didn't need to anchor again and there were no more rivers to navigate.

While on vacation at home I received my report card for the cruise—it showed an A in both Navigation and Rules of the Road, a B for Seamanship, but I got another C in watch standing, just like the last time. But now it was getting close to being my final year at the academy, and that meant graduation wasn't too far off. There was no stopping me now!

4

When I Graduate

After my spring break ended in 1984, I returned back to the academy with the stress of another cruise under my belt. It was good knowing I'd soon be a first-class midshipman after this semester ended, and that couldn't happen soon enough. Then my economics teacher called me into his office and told me he was expanding the tutoring lab. I was still wondering how he knew the success of it though, as there was never anyone from the academy staff coming in when we had the lab open. A cadet once brought me a difficult question even though he already had the answer—did my economics teacher put him up to that? But all the students who came in were only fourth-class cadets anyways, so the questions they had weren't too difficult to answer. I was happy though, and how my teacher knew didn't really matter to me.

On occasions when I had breaks in-between my regular classes, I would often go to my favorite place to study, which happened to be the campus library. It was a large building situated below the assembly area, and inside the library were the latest newspapers and magazines, including an extensive collection of every nautical book ever written. The chairs arranged along the back windows offered beautiful views of the nearby straits where the shipping traffic navigated past our campus on a daily basis.

Some interesting things were seen while I was seated there; from small sailboats to large tankers passing by our campus. On one occasion I even saw the U.S. Coast Guard searching for someone who'd jumped off the Carquinez Bridge to commit suicide. The waters around the bridge were narrowed into a strong current that always flowed out to sea. Not only had I sailed by the bridge many times in the afternoon using sailboats, but also as part of our training where we practiced docking with a supply boat. As the Coast Guard searched under the bridge for a body, they would go to one side of the strait and look there, and then try the other side before going back again. But they always stayed right around the bridge and didn't follow the current downstream. If the person had jumped from the center span, their body must have drifted out to the distant point and beyond, while the Coast Guard was still looking under the bridge.

Another time I saw a tugboat headed upstream towing a large barge behind it that was sinking. I could see the barge was slowly listing to one side, and the further it got pulled up the channel, the deeper it sank into the water. Eventually the tugboat moved over to the far shoreline and waited while it slipped under, then they released the tow cable and the barge disappeared. No markers were dropped and I imagine it's still there at the bottom of the straits just west of the academy.

When a month passed after returning to campus, a tug pushing a barge came up the straits with a crane on its deck—along with an anchor and ten shots of chain sitting next to it. This was to replace what we'd lost in the Columbia River. I'd assumed someone would salvage the old anchor from the river and bring it back to us, instead this one was different. Once they secured the crane to the training ship, the new chain was pulled through the hawse pipe and connected down in the chain locker, then they used the windlass to raise the rest of the chain and finally they secured the anchor. Cadets were busy painting it to match its neighbor on the starboard side, but it was obvious to anyone who looked carefully—the two anchors were a mismatched pair, at least with the flukes having different shapes. Cadets in later years must've wondered what happened to the anchors, and why they were both different looking on the bow of the training ship.

I continued working in the tutoring lab and attending classes in Electrical Equipment Operations, Navigation, Rules of the Road, Applied Seamanship, and International Law while at the academy. And after I made it through those classes, that started my last year of schooling. The end was in sight!

For the Fall semester I had classes in Meteorology, Admiralty Law, Seamanship, Communications, Piloting lab, and Navigation. Being a first-class midshipman also meant there were more freedoms while on campus, such as being able to wear my hair longer. It was surprising how I got away with it, the same length would've been twenty-five demerits a few semesters earlier, but not now. And maybe the excitement of this being my last year made me study less, since I barely broke a B average, yet it didn't matter. I knew what lay ahead before graduating—just one more cruise and then the licensing seminars.

Then at the end of the semester the academy informed me that I'd be sailing as a cadet aboard an oil tanker, instead of going on the training ship again. What a relief! I'd already done two trips aboard the Golden Bear and was ready for something new. They gave me instructions on when to call the ship's agent in charge of scheduling when the time came. It was great news to hear, and I was excited to see how the maritime industry outside of the academy worked—this was my big opportunity.

When I called the ship's agent just before the new year, he told me that I'd be sailing on one of their crude oil tankers running on the West Coast. The ship loaded crude oil in Alaska and then sailed to Panama, where her cargo was discharged. Then it was back to Alaska to load up for another run. Since the ship would be anchoring in the Port of Los Angeles on the way north, that's where new crewmembers and supplies would be loaded. He then told me the date and time I was to be there, and to fly down to LAX and go to the loading pier, where I'd take a launch out to the ship at the anchorage. He also casually mentioned that I'd have to cross some picket lines to get past the entrance, but not to worry. Apparently the deck officer's union went on strike for higher wages, while the company wanted them lowered. It didn't sound like a happy situation, but I wanted to see the real world, and this was every bit of that.

When the big day arrived for my trip, I was packed and ready with everything in my sea bag. Once I boarded the airplane, it was a short flight down from there, and around noon we landed at the LAX airport in Los Angeles, where I got into a taxi and told the driver the pier number at the harbor. It seemed quite a drive to get out there, but eventually we took some turns after getting off the freeway, and headed to where there were views of the water-front.

The taxi driver hit the side road and went down one street, and then another. As he came to the pier at the end, that's when I saw the picket lines. They had some union signs resting along the chain link fence at the entrance to the pier, along with union members standing around holding up more signs. As I got closer, they quickly saw my taxi pulling up.

"Here's one coming!" I heard shouted.

"It's another scab! You won't be boarding today!"

I had changed into my academy uniform earlier while in the airport bathroom, hoping to be taken as a neutral observer by any roughnecks. And luckily it worked. Between my uniform and my CMA sea bag with the insignia on it, they figured out I was only a cadet.

"False alarm! He's only a cadet."

"Say hi to the scabs when you get aboard, Cadet! Tell them we're out here waiting for them!"

And with that I was through. I breathed a sign of relief and proceeded to the launch area, where I got on the launch and named the ship I needed. Quickly I was taken out to the anchorage where they had the ship's gangway lowered. As the launch pulled up to the ship at anchor, I jumped onto the landing platform, then walked up the gangway while carrying my sea bag over my shoulder.

The first thing I noticed was how huge the ship appeared when stepping off onto her main deck. She was quite a ways out of the water while under ballast, since this was the return trip where she carried no crude oil. As I later found out, she was 906 feet long with a beam (width) of 173 feet, and drew fifty-five feet of water when loaded. She could carry 1.2 million barrels of crude oil, and sailed at nearly sixteen knots.

I made my way towards the stern where the main house was located that contained the berthing areas, the bridge and eating quarters. After going through a lower hatch, I went up to try and find the captain. Compared to the training ship, this place seemed deserted, but eventually I bumped into another crewmember. He directed me up to the deck just below the bridge, which apparently was the captain's deck.

Once up top I met the captain, who seemed very nice and signed me on. He told me the ship would only be anchored long enough to change out the crew and load supplies along with bunkers, then we'd raise the anchor and sail for Valdez. Since this was early winter, that probably meant a rough trip through the Gulf of Alaska, before making our way into Prince William Sound, and finally over to the Valdez loading docks.

The next day we departed and I was added to the morning deck gang with the bosun from 8:00 a.m. to noontime, and then stood watch up on the bridge with the chief mate from 4:00 p.m. to 8:00 p.m. The academy had given me a long list of items to complete for the trip, which included schematics, navigation, cargo operations, rules of the road, and communication projects. I quickly found out that the deck officers were the only ones who were non-union aboard the ship, the rest of the crew was union— but accepted them as legitimate crewmembers. Sometimes a union will honor another union's strike and not work in sympathy, but that wasn't the case here.

The bosun was an interesting character that was in charge of the deck gang, and we did whatever work he was told to do by the chief mate. He must've started sailing back during World War II as he was in his 60's now, and his arms were full of the old sailor tattoos that had faded over many years of sun and aging. I quickly found out he liked to smoke marijuana, along with the other A/B's to pass the time while working. This was done during every coffee break we had, the group of them would go into a storage room and light up a joint, then puff it down and go back out to work again. I was compelled to join them once in doing this, just to be part of the gang. How they didn't have a raging headache by the end of the day, I don't know, but they smoked a lot of marijuana, and that included the pumpman along with them.

The pumpman was in charge of keeping the cargo pumps, cargo valves, and cargo pipelines aboard in perfect working order. At times during this trip I'd also work alongside him. We might change out the expansion fittings on the main pipelines running along the cargo deck, or do some work down in the pumproom itself depending on the weather. There was always something to do that needed attention aboard such a large ship. This was all easy work to do, cutting off old bolts and replacing them with new bolts. There were thousands of bolts that needed this, so the pumpman had a never-ending job of it.

Eventually we made it up the Pacific Coast into the large fog banks that formed offshore in winter, and stuck around for days on end. It could be so thick that we might not be able to see one mile ahead or even the bow of the ship from the bridge, so all the mates could do was watch the radar and listen for any ship's whis-tles. But we never slowed down due to the thick fog, it was always full-speed ahead right through it. This fog lasted until we hit the stronger winds as we neared Alaska, along with the heavy seas they formed. One interesting thing I noticed was how the ship flexed in the swells during a storm. While standing at one end of the ship, I could see her twisting as she moved through the ocean, it was almost scary in a way.

The strongest storms could become quite dangerous, and we hit one early on that pounded against the bow with its massive seas. When this happened, the captain slowed the ship just enough so that this pounding stopped, otherwise it might actually crack the ship's hull. The spray that resulted from this pounding could shoot hundreds of feet up into the air, and at times if it was windy enough—it could even hit the bridge almost 800 feet away.

I had the feeling that if anything happened in one of these big storms, we'd have little chance of surviving a sinking. The temper-atures were in the 40's, and the winds might be blowing fifty to sixty knots outside. Just to launch a lifeboat would be extremely difficult under those circumstances, then to get in one and somehow survive aboard it on these crashing waves? I knew such a thing would be hopeless, but that's the risk we took when going so far north in the winter.

As we approached Prince William Sound, ice started to form on the forward part of the ship from the spray blowing over the bow constantly. It started to cover everything it landed on, unless it was getting hit so much that the seawater melted it away. Before hitting port, I went out with the deck gang to use sledgehammers and knock off as much as we could in the working areas for safety reasons.

Inside Prince William Sound, we followed the traffic separation scheme laid out on the chart for the area, with its shipping lanes for northern or southern traffic to follow. We passed by Bligh Reef and the Columbia Glacier, which was shedding icebergs into the shipping lanes at times. We safely made it by this area and picked up the pilot, who came aboard to take us into Port Valdez and the Alyeska pipeline terminal.

Fortunately the weather forecast was for a light overcast with slight snow flurries possible, and since it was January, it was very cold outside when we docked. While on deck I wore a body suit that was insulated and kept me warm, except for the face, it was just too cold to wear regular pants and a jacket outside. After we tied up, the first thing they did was have a small tender pull a boom around the ship in case there was an oil spill. When looking over the side, I could see quite a ways into the water, it looked so crystal clear and pristine it was amazing. The operation they had at the terminal was strictly business, they moved like clockwork to get the ship ready for loading, then finished and out of port so the next one could quickly be tied up and the process started over again.

Off in the distance to the east I could see what was left of the old town of Valdez that was destroyed by a tsunami in 1964, the result of the Good Friday earthquake. This was the most powerful earthquake ever recorded in the United States, registering a magnitude of 9.2 on the Richter scale.

Once they were nearly ready to start loading, I went ashore with the second mate to go into the new Valdez—it's where the town was moved about four miles away to a safer location. But I couldn't believe how cold it was ashore, it seemed even frostier in town than it was on the ship, and here we were going to the post office. I also noticed there weren't any wild animals walking around along the roads, even they knew how to stay warm and hidden away safely.

We didn't stay long in town, as the second mate had to get back and be ready for watch soon, but I gained a lot of respect for those who lived in Alaska, especially through a long, cold winter. I was glad to leave and head back to the ship, with the thought of a cold beer in town being the last thing I needed, especially since the Sun was barely up for a few hours, and then dipped so low on the horizon it was easy to miss.

After we got back to the ship, they'd already started loading the crude oil. The chief mate was in the control room where they had a large panel showing a schematic of the ship's tanks along with colored switches to control the many valves. There were also controls for the main cargo pumps, and an indicator for the trim of the ship. Readings were shown that gave the cargo levels for each tank as well. As we loaded the crude oil, they had to keep the ship trimmed so she didn't list to one side or the other, and also so she remained deeper in the water towards the stern. One time we accidentally let her get trimmed down by the bow, and the captain wasn't happy with us. Everything in the engine room was designed to flow back, and when trimmed the other way, things could stop working for the engineers.

As the sky outside turned to darkness, the oil terminal itself remained lit up like it was daylight, since they had huge halogen lamps broadcasting all around the platforms for safety. One interesting thing was how warm the crude oil measured when loading, with the cargo temperatures being close to ninety degrees Fahrenheit. And as a light snow started falling outside, the warm tanks melted it away and kept the main deck clear for us to walk on.

Since oil expands and contracts based on its temperature, when crude oil is at ninety degrees, it takes up more volume than if it was at forty degrees. That's why it was important to have exact temperature readings on the crude oil being loaded, as they had to calculate the amount based on the industry standard at sixty degrees, which was used to determine a barrel of oil for purchase or sale. So once the cargo was adjusted from ninety degrees to sixty degrees, that was the official loaded quantity we carried aboard.

Of course they also had to discharge the segregated ballast water being carried, and that had actually started earlier out at sea, so there was less to offload through the segregated ballast system. That was completed prior to finishing the loading, which came in at a rate of almost 100,000 barrels of crude oil per hour. Since the ship carried nearly 1.2 million barrels, it was finished in approximately fourteen hours, not including our maneuvering and preparation time.

The first tanks to be topped off were the after tanks, and then they topped off the tanks going forward until they were finished with them all. This was done to maintain the ship's trim, and the finished tanks ended up being nearly full—all were loaded to within a few feet from the top of the tanks, which surprised me.

Before we left port, the captain asked the second mate for a head count to make sure we sailed with a full crew. After checking, everyone was accounted for, even the pumpman who'd run into one of the steel mooring cables while stoned. He had a big gash across his bloody nose, but they never asked him to explain it. And they didn't bother checking on the Steward's department, since the captain said never mind when asked. If one of them had missed the trip, we'd get along fine without him.

Once we got back out to sea, the ship seemed to ride much better than when under ballast. And since we were now headed more southerly, the storms were generally at our backs as we rode along with them. That was much more pleasant than fighting them on the way in. Also the tanker acted more like a submarine at times when we occasionally took waves over the deck as we rode through some of it. You definitely didn't want to be walking on the main deck when that happens. The captain would close off the deck to any crewmembers for safety. It would take something urgent to allow someone to try and make it forward with waves crashing and rolling down there.

And this did happen on one day, when they received a bilge alarm warning coming from up forward in the focsle. This meant the bow might be taking on water, and that was a very urgent situation to fix. The captain was up on the bridge while he sent the chief mate and the pumpman forward to check on the alarm as huge waves occasionally came down the main deck. Luckily they made it all the way forward without coming close to being hit, then they reported it was a false alarm, so the captain sent them back.

This they tried to do quickly, and they made it back along the entire length of the ship without a wave coming close, until they crossed to go towards the ladder on the port side of the house. That's where a large wave got the chief mate and threw him against one of the steel breakwaters. But somehow he didn't get washed overboard, and recovered in time to get off the main deck before the next wave hit. Had he gone into the ocean under those sea conditions, we never would've found him. The pumpman could only watch from above, not being able to do anything without risking his own life.

Once we got out of the rough seas, we ended up heading back through the fog banks again, and then after a few days of bad visibility, we eventually make it out into the better weather along the California coast. Since the entire run south to Panama would be about twenty days to complete, when we added in the time to head north to Valdez, each round trip took a month and a half to finish. I was scheduled to do two round trips while aboard, for a total of three months sailing time as a cadet.

As we continued farther south into warmer waters, we eventually passed by the resorts of Cabo San Lucas, Manzanillo and Acapulco, then finally started to enter the Gulf of Tehuantepec. Few people outside of sailors know about the dangers of this gulf due to its unique geography. A narrow gap in the mountain range ashore allows inland winds to blow through it, usually in the early afternoon, and these can become gale, or even hurricane force winds. Once out over the Gulf of Tehuantepec, they quickly build up some heavy seas in the process. Anyone caught off guard is either blown well off course as a result, or even risks a possible sinking.

We were lucky and made it through the area without incident, then continued on past Costa Rica until we arrived at the crude oil discharge station. This terminal in Panama was developed to bypass the Panama Canal due to the size limitation of the shipping locks. Once we discharged ashore at the oil terminal, the crude oil was held in large storage tanks nearby, and then pumped across Panama using an eighty mile long pipeline, where it arrived on the Caribbean coast—to be loaded there into other oil tankers and then sailed north to Texas. But even this pipeline run might not be permanent, as there was talk of a pipeline from California to Texas being built, so as to cut this trip short. But until that happened, this longer run to Panama was still necessary, which meant more money for the shipping companies.

The offshore terminal in Panama used a local crew to tie us up, while the piping we were to discharge through was submerged underwater and ran up onto the beach and out into the distance. Once the ship was securely tied up to the offshore bollards, we raised the piping connectors with the booms to secure them at the manifold. When discharging the crude oil, we used the ship's cargo pumps to accomplish this, and they were also used to strip the last amounts of cargo out as well. This was generally done in the reverse order of loading. We needed to take the cargo out evenly, but the forward tanks were emptied out faster to keep the ship trimmed properly. Eventually, they said, the ballasting would begin.

After we started operations, I was allowed to go ashore and see the area by myself in the afternoon. They had a launch that took me to the dock by the beach, which led to the outer gate where there was a taxi waiting outside. This was driven by one of the local Panamanians who spoke decent enough English. Once inside the taxi, he told me everything that was available in the area, from groceries to drinking, and from women to Cocaina. It wasn't hard to figure out what the last item was, but instead I decided to take a trip to the red zone. He offered to take me there and wait while I was busy, then drive me for the return trip back to the ship. I got the feeling he did this quite a lot, so I went along with his suggestion.

The jungle roads we went along reminded me of those by the coast in Zihuatanejo, where they all looked alike. It was also hard to tell which direction we were headed in, but we finally stopped at a small place towards the crest of a hill and got out somewhere in the jungle. I entered the bar along with the taxi driver, and was surprised to see the place nearly empty. The bartender was over at the long serving area with empty stools, but there were a couple of young whores hanging out at a different table across the room. Then a lone soul came out of one of the back rooms, and he was a fellow American. He walked over and talked with one of the two whores, but acted very nervous. Maybe he was afraid I'd tell his wife about him, since he forgot to take off that shiny wedding ring from his finger—then he quickly disappeared outside.

I ordered a beer for myself and had one sent over to the taxi driver, who was hanging out at a different table and acting like he belonged there, while the two hookers came over to see what I wanted. Both of them were fairly young and pretty, and as I drank my beer, we talked a bit. I talked more with the brunette, eventually going back with her after agreeing on a price. I found out this place was much more casual than the one in Panama City. After we'd undressed and started, I didn't hear any knocks on the door to let me know when my time was almost up. This was more relaxing than trying to finish in a hurry. I guess the bartender didn't care, maybe they got paid the same no matter how long it took. With me being her only customer, they probably wanted me to stick around as long as possible perhaps.

After we finished, I asked to use the bathroom and was shown a door by the back wall. It didn't take long to figure out the place had no sewage treatment installed, not even a septic system. There was an opening in the bathroom wall meant to be a window, and when I flushed the toilet and looked out, I saw it went straight out into a ditch that ran away from the building. It was the same with the other nearby rooms as well, they all flushed down the same ditch towards a ravine, where the toilet paper and everything else was piling up.

After I tipped the bartender on the way out, my taxi driver asked me where to go next, and I mentioned wanting to purchase a small amount of Cocaina to help me stay awake at times. He nodded and drove me over to a small house where a guy sold me one hundred dollars worth. That was more than I wanted, but it was the minimum I could buy. So having that he drove me back through the jungle roads to the dock, where I tipped the driver and thanked him for escorting me around, mentioning I might be back on my next round trip.

Since I'd only been gone for a few hours, when I boarded the ship they were still discharging the crude oil, with many hours left to go until it was finished. This was done from inside the control room, where the pump and valve controls were located. I needed to get the details of the whole operation written down for my cruise notebook, being the main project to complete for this trip, just as I'd done when loading in Valdez. There were other sections to complete about the piping systems, fire systems, cargo capacities, navigation, rules of the road, ship handling, seamanship and safety gear. It was better to get it finished as soon as possible rather than leave it all for later.

The following afternoon we finished discharging and ballasting the tanker, so we departed the terminal and headed north for the Port of Los Angeles. After a couple of days out at sea, I decided to try out some of the Cocaina and learned a hard lesson about how powerful it was. While I didn't know it at the time, when the stuff normally makes it into the U.S. market, it has been "cut" a few times—which means it was thinned out to make it more bulky and valuable. The Cocaina that I'd purchased must have never been "cut", so it was extremely powerful. I took a few lines of it in the early evening and within a couple of minutes it nearly sent me over the side of the ship! It was like being hit by a locomotive at full speed, my heart started racing about a million beats a minute. Was I going to die?

I panicked and dumped all the Cocaina into the toilet and flushed it down. No way was I going to be found dead with this stuff in my cabin. My heart raced on and off for a few hours and into the early morning, until my body finally came down from its high. Eventually I passed out and slept for a day, and didn't leave my cabin for another day after that.

When I finally left to go up to the bridge and pretend like I'd been busy working on my cruise notebook, by chance I saw the captain in the passageway. He said to me in a kidding manner, "There you are, I was wondering what happened to you. We

57

thought you might have died." For some reason I found that to be very funny, it was like he'd hit the nail on the head. But that was it for me, I never told anyone about this experience while on the ship or afterwards, and I never touched that stuff again, having learned my lesson about its power the hard way.

At the Port of Los Angeles we anchored in the harbor for a crew change, and among those coming aboard was a third-class cadet from the U.S. Merchant Marine Academy at King's Point. He was scheduled to stay on the ship for three months, or two round trips, and along with the crew changes we also loaded some fresh supplies for the rest of the trip north. I even met the ship's agent briefly, he was aboard to talk with the captain about the last voyage, and to collect the ship's paperwork. Once everything was completed, we departed that afternoon, on our way up to Valdez.

Sometimes at sea I would take a stroll out on deck alone, and by chance I went out that evening after we'd left port to watch the lights on the California coast. As I walked up forward on the ship's main deck, I saw the new cadet sitting on one of the ballast pipes midway up the starboard side. I walked up to him and asked what he was up to. He gave me a sigh and said how he was reflecting at night about his problems and trying to decide something about school and how to proceed.

Then I said, "No, I mean what are you doing smoking out on deck?"

Aboard the ship they had signs stenciled everywhere, including coming out of every hatch and doorway, which said—NO SMOKING—in large letters, with ashtrays nearby to leave the cigarettes behind. And on the outside of the main house facing forward in huge red letters were the words—NO SMOKING. It was almost impossible to miss these warnings. Instead, he said to me, "Oh, I had no idea," and he casually put out the lit cigarette. That's when I pointed back to the big letters, "Can't you read the words on the front of the house? You could have BLOWN US ALL UP!" And with that I left him alone, hoping it put some sense into him.

I continued to work on my cruise notebook as we went through the fog banks, rough weather, and eventually we made it up to

Alaska. I was still standing watches and working with the deck gang, and after we loaded and left to head south, the same rough weather greeted us again in the Gulf of Alaska. But eventually it turned to nice weather when we got to the California coast again, where the chief mate decided to synchronize the tank gauging system. These were the sensors at each tank that gave us the digital readouts in the control room used for loading and discharging. If these readings were off it might cause an oil spill, however, being a cadet—I had no idea how to do it, and only assisted him.

At the first tank he used a resistance meter on the sensor readings, then had me twist the screws on the back of each unit until it gave the correct readout. There were two sensors for each tank—one used for gauging the entire depth of the tank, while the other was used when topping off. We did this for each of the cargo and ballast tanks on the entire ship, taking a few days to complete them all. And then a couple of days later, the first assistant engineer came to me complaining about how we'd stolen his overtime. It wasn't our business to even touch those sensors, he said, it was the engineer's job only. I wisely didn't say anything back being only a lowly cadet on the ship, while the engineers were all paid union members.

But the engineers weren't the only crewmembers unhappy as I found out a few days later. While I was alone on deck in the afternoon, the bosun happened to walk up to me by himself and stopped for a moment. He looked at me and said the deck crew was unhappy with how the chief mate was treating them. The deck crew—meaning him and the six A/B's. He mumbled something about why they were unhappy, then said they might have to take care of him. And then he looked at me and said if I happened to be working with the chief mate when that happened, they wouldn't be leaving any witnesses.

Then he walked away and didn't look back.

Did I hear that right? It sounded to me like he'd just threatened to kill the chief mate, and me if I was with him. I thought for a moment and let it sink in, then came to the obvious conclusion that yes, that's what he'd just told me.

That led me to the next question. So what should I do about it?

That was a very complicated one to answer, as I didn't doubt for a second that the bosun was capable of doing it. In fact, I would bet that he'd probably done it in the past just by the looks of him, he seemed to be an old salt coming through the roughest of times. But there were only two people who I could tell this to—either the captain or the chief mate.

Then I realized what would happen if I did that. They would confront the bosun, and that meant he would know I was the one who squealed. Under those circumstances, it would really become quite dangerous on the ship for me. It was already dangerous now after his threat, but it would even be more so if I talked.

So I decided to go with the least dangerous route and say nothing—not anything to the chief mate, and especially nothing to the captain.

While the chief mate was a big guy capable of defending himself, he was no reason for me to die over. And I think I made the right decision to this day as there was the slight chance the bosun was just testing me somehow. I doubt it was that simple, but it wasn't beyond the realm of possibilities. Of course I'd never know as nothing ever happened to the chief mate while I was on the ship, and as I'd learn later, he would eventually sail as a captain.

So after all this excitement, I really didn't need any more. Lucky for me the rest of the trip went smoothly while I laid low; still focusing on finishing my cruise notebook, then making it safely off the ship in Los Angeles harbor. Before leaving, I put on my academy uniform for the trip out, knowing I still had to cross the union picket lines. And sure enough, when I made it out with the launch and onto the loading pier, they yelled asking me how the scabs aboard were, and of course I ignored them while getting into the taxi. But as I found out later, the company eventually won and those guys never returned to work—their union had been broken.

For my last semester at the academy, I returned from vacation to begin the licensing seminars being held for those of us graduating. These were meant to refresh us on every topic needed for the licensing exams, plus we were later to take mock up exams to get us ready for the real testing. There was also the required physical to show we were fit enough to be seamen, so in order to get that out of the way as soon as possible, I went with four of my friends to the designated medical building located by the waterfront in San Francisco.

On a sunny day we parked just off the Bay Bridge on the east side of the city, and noticed after we got out of the car a messenger delivering a package to the building across the street. When he parked his bicycle and went inside, one of the guys sitting outside jumped on it and rode off. By the time the messenger came out screaming for someone to stop the thief, he'd already pedaled beyond the street corner and was hopelessly gone. We continued on in disbelief, eventually going into the secure facility for the physical given by a doctor. This meant we had to change out of our khaki uniforms, and someone working inside the building knew that. After we'd finished and put on our uniforms, one of my friends noticed all of his money was missing from his wallet. That was strike two. If that wasn't enough, they had broken into the car we came in as well. This was discovered after we returned to drive back to the academy, giving us an unforgettable trip to be sure.

Near the end of the semester, the U.S. Coast Guard came out to the academy to test us officially for our licenses. That happened over a couple week's worth of testing, and nerves were high for all of us. In the end though any cadet who failed a section was allowed to retry it until they passed. So all of us made it through, and that meant we'd finally graduate together on May 25th, 1985. The end was in sight!

The morning of graduation, we put on our black dress uniforms, shined our shoes, and headed down to assembly, where we'd march together for a grand entrance in front of all of our friends and families who came to see us. I happened to be walking across by the flagpole when the head commandant came up and told me my coat was buttoned backwards. Only three years earlier he'd nearly had me kicked out for upsetting that bar owner, and how long ago that seemed. I thanked him and continued on, getting into position with the rest of the cadets.

After everyone was ready and lined up, we started marching together and walked up the main road, making our way towards the seats arranged just in front of the stage set up on the grass. The Mariners Choir was singing a chorus during our entrance, while all the spectators were waving and taking pictures of us. Among them I spotted my parents, my two grandmothers, and my sister holding her small son dressed in a sailor's suit. We continued on and took our places among the arranged chairs—then we all sat down together at the same time—and the graduation ceremony was started. First an invocation was given at the podium by the local Pastor, followed by a speech from our California state senator—then we got to the presentations of awards.

We were conferred our Bachelor of Science degrees by the chairperson of the Board of Governors, a Coast Guard licensing oath was given by a U.S. Coast Guard Captain, and a commissioning oath for the Naval Reserve was given by the Admiral.

Finally the big moment came—when one by one—each of us walked up and received our diplomas while shaking hands with the presenting Admiral. Everyone in the audience clapped for each cadet as we passed through, and once we were all finished, a benediction was given. At the end came the magic words we'd all waited four years to hear—*You've officially graduated.* Upon hearing this we stood up together and threw our white hats as far into the air as we could, and with that my time at the California Maritime Academy was over. I was a Maritime Academy Graduate!

5

To Work At Sea

By the time of my graduation, I'd sent out dozens of resumes to nearly all of the shipping companies—just as the other graduates had done from each of the three maritime academies. But at this time the industry was at rock bottom with few jobs available, and those few were probably going to relatives of people already in the industry. Eventually I had a whole stack of rejection letters in a folder at home, all from the companies that had received my resume and had given me back responses similar to these ones:

Dear Mr. Glissmeyer,

This will acknowledge receipt of your letter requesting employment in the capacity of a Third Mate.

Unfortunately, we must advise you that we currently have an excess of personnel due to the sale of many of our vessels caused by the depressed tanker market. Additionally, we have a long waiting list of qualified applications for the few vessels remaining.

Dear Mr. Glissmeyer,

Thank you for your interest in our tanker fleet. Due to the continuing depressed oil market, I must advise you that our company is not presently hiring additional personnel for our vessels. Therefore, we are advising you that we will not be inviting you in for an interview.

Dear Mr. Glissmeyer,

Thank you for submitting your resume to our corporate office.

We wish that job requirements were such that we could consider all those that have recently sent a resume to our company. We regret that we cannot give you any encouragement at this time.

Dear Mr. Glissmeyer,

Thank you for your recent inquiry regarding employment opportunities with our company.

We have reviewed our needs carefully and find that we do not have an opening available which matches your abilities and qualifications. We will retain your resume for one year and contact you should a suitable opening occur.

Dear. Mr. Glissmeyer,

Thank you for your inquiry regarding possible employment in our maritime business.

The information you provided has been reviewed by employment professionals. As you could well expect, we have many more applicants than we have openings. Because of this situation, we are not in a position to hire additional personnel.

The other rejection letters in my folder went on and on similar to these ones; some were worded close to the same, a few talked about overbooked union crews and mentioned where to apply elsewhere (good-luck with that). Based on this it wasn't hard to figure out why so few of us graduating were even getting jobs at sea, much less being hired as third mates.

A year later, I got together with my fellow 2-D graduates who lived in the area for a drink to reminisce, and all of them were in the same situation I was. A few others had decided to enter directly into the U.S. Navy from the academy, and they were gladly accepted. But other than that, the industry seemed dead for jobs, at least to outsiders like us with no connections.

That's when I decided to go back to school to become an electrical engineer, and took classes at our local community colleges. Eventually I had taken enough credits to successfully enter San Jose State University. So off to the university I went, thinking I had everything ready to be accepted. I drove to one of the large parking garages they had just outside of the admissions area. When I pulled inside, there was a guy who saw me park my car and didn't say anything—he was an attendant at the garage. I assumed since he saw me, it was OK to park there. From there I crossed the campus and talked to the admission's department.

They gave me some information and I handed over all of my class credits from both the community college courses and the California Maritime Academy. Then I left and made it back to my parked car, which had a ticket on the windshield. That guy had given me a parking ticket instead of telling me I couldn't park there!

Naturally he wouldn't take back the ticket. This was so wrong, but what else could I do, so I left and wrote a letter to the judge who was in charge of appeals. In it I explained how the guy never said a word about my parking place even though he saw me do it, and I was there trying to get admitted as a new student. Fortunately the judge cancelled the ticket, so there was some justice in San Jose after all.

Unfortunately, I didn't have the same luck with the admission's department. They wouldn't accept enough of the classes I'd taken at the academy for my general education requirements. That left me needing to complete classes in advanced writing, speech, biology, fine arts, and behavioral sciences, which added another year of classes just to be admitted as a transfer student. And then it was another two years to do the engineering classes to graduate. It was overwhelming and I was flabbergasted at my bad luck.

I did a couple of odd jobs in the meantime, one was working as a handyman for a trucking company. I did do some trucking work, but mostly worked on houses to fix them up for sale for the owner's own benefit. I quit that job and even tried a small hand at beekeeping of all things, but that wasn't anything serious. I also looked into becoming an air traffic controller, but it sounded like a long process to complete for a seemingly stressful job.

That's when I decided to try and work at sea again, but this time it would be different. No longer would I flood the industry with resumes. No need to send them to those that weren't hiring, right? I needed to send them to those that were hiring. For starters, I had decided to take any job at sea at this point, as I hadn't been out on a ship for a few years, and to go on as a third mate now seemed about as likely as being hired as an astronaut by NASA.

Instead, I used the maritime academy resources and found a couple of companies that were possibilities. These weren't for jobs as a third mate, but were openings for A/B's (able-bodied seamen). When I thought about it, the time I'd spent at the academy was very much like being an able-bodied seaman, so what was so bad about going back and sailing as one?

I selected the companies and carefully sent out a resume to each of them. Then a couple of letters came back as rejections, until I got one like this:

Dear Mr. Glissmeyer,

Thank you very much for sending your resume to our employment office where we coordinate all the training for our licensed personnel. You have outstanding qualifications and we will try to obtain an opening for you on one of our ships.

Your resume has been forwarded to our corporate office for further processing. If you would consider sailing as an A/B while your security clearance is being processed, please feel free to contact us as we have some openings coming up in late May and early June.

Late May or early June? When was my letter mailed to me? At the top of the letter it said the 13th of May, 1988, meaning job openings would become available in only a week or two.

Hurray!!!!!!!!! I'd finally found a job!!!!!!!!!!!

I quickly called the company and did everything they asked of me. To begin with they had me take a couple of classes at a military base in Oakland, California. The first was a course in weapons training, where they took me along with some other trainees up to a gun range above the nearby cliffs, and they gave us safety training along with having us shoot the various weapons we might have aboard our ship. That also included launching a mortar shell at a target down the longest area of the range. Of course it was very fun to do this class—automatic weapons and a mortar shell, what wasn't there to like about that?

The other class I attended was in nuclear fallout, and there I was the only trainee needing to be certified on this topic. The instructor talked for about half an hour on nuclear radiation and how it would affect people aboard a ship, until eventually he started to get angry that I wasn't taking notes as he lectured me. I knew this class wasn't meant as a test, it was only for an education on the subject, so I didn't feel the need to be writing down what he said. Towards the end I asked him if a crew could stop the radiation from harming us due to a nearby nuclear strike, and his answer back was no, we couldn't stop it. He only mentioned treating everyone after the fact, and since we'd be out at sea while being stuck in the radiation, there was no escaping it. That meant we'd all probably die on the ship, and it didn't take notes to remember that one.

Once these classes were finished, the next week I was packed and on a plane flight out to Hawaii, with a destination of Hickam Air Force Base. In the brochure I read during the plane flight, it explained what the training I'd taken was for, and it also explained the company's operations. It said they were responsible for manning five ships out of Pearl Harbor that were part of something called the SURTASS platform, an undersea surveillance system. The ships were entirely crewed by civilian employees, but were under contract with the U.S. Navy.

While in port the personnel were to wear standard working uniforms so as to blend in with the rest of the naval ships in the area. That meant dungarees for the unlicensed personnel and khakis for the licensed crewmembers, including the bosun. They recommended that crewmembers adapt to a 180 days at sea and 90 days off schedule, but promised to be flexible about it.

Towards the end they also stated how this program gave valuable experience and insight to enhance and broaden one's career. Whereas other aspects of the merchant industry were struggling for survival, the operation of these vessels for the government allowed for a growing field of opportunity for steady employment and advancements in one's career.

If crewmembers wanted to receive mail while aboard, they had to use the Navy Fleet post office address, since the next port of call was usually classified prior to each mission. The ships were operated for extended periods without hitting port for up to seventy-five days, so no mail would be received during those long stretches at sea.

They mentioned that they were confident how all the crewmembers would be pleased by the fine selection of tasty food that the steward's department would be preparing for us when aboard the ship. Because of the small size of the crews, all meals would be served cafeteria style, meaning that each individual would take his plate to the galley to be served. Despite the limited amount of storage space and the long mission periods, they claimed to still be able to serve at least two entrees at each meal. The food would be plentiful and tasty they said—I hoped they were right.

No alcohol was allowed aboard the ship though, and anyone who was caught with alcohol would be reprimanded by the captain. That also included non-prescribed narcotics, which the captain could search for if he suspected, and anything found would be permanently seized.

The firefighting equipment was promised to be the best available, and we'd have scheduled drills to learn how to operate and store it safely in case we had to use it in an emergency. There would be quarterly drills in man overboard, wash downs for chemical and biological defense, and line throwing appliance drills. Weekly we should expect drills for fire and lifeboats, and also in damage control.

We weren't to bring cameras for photographing any of the ship's operations, especially when the array was being deployed, towed, or retrieved. It did say that besides the regular crewmembers, there would be seven civilian technicians aboard who operated the electronics for the array system, and they'd be considered separate from the crew. This use of civilians on U.S. Navy ships was mentioned as growing, at that time it comprised a total of 123 U.S. Navy ships, up from 78 only four years earlier.

Then they thanked me for joining the team, and looked forward to seeing everyone aboard the ship. Wow, I thought, I hope it's as good as they say. I guess I'll find out soon enough. So after the plane landed and I made it outside of the airport on Oahu, I took a taxi out as instructed to the air base, and that's where I saw my first ship tied up at the dock.

She was a small TAGOS vessel that was being used to listen for Soviet submarines during the Cold War. The ship was painted a bright white, and was moored at the entrance to Pearl Harbor on a long pier that stretched off from the shoreline. She was 224 feet long with a beam (width) of 43 feet, and used a twin-screw diesel electric plant to run things. As I climbed aboard her, I noticed how the hull looked like it was made of welded sheets of plywood. That's pretty odd. I guess that meant the metal was very thin, and if they scrimped on the hull, I wondered what else they scrimped on in building her?

I also knew when I took this job that the pay was next to nothing, it amounted to only forty dollars a day for twelve hour days, seven days a week. Could they really pay that low?

But I didn't care—as I had a job—and that was all that mattered.

Once aboard the ship I could see the Honolulu shoreline off in the distance, and in the other direction were some U.S. Navy ships moored along some nearby piers, while the Arizona Memorial could be seen beyond those with its American flag waving high above it. I couldn't believe how incredible this was! I'd seen this place only in war movies like *Tora! Tora! Tora!*, and in a couple of others, but it was more breathtaking to see it here in real life!

On the ship I noticed how the crewmembers were wearing dungarees for the unlicensed personnel and khakis for the officers, just like it said in the brochure. I went into the berthing area and found the captain, who took my papers and also my third mate's license, then signed me on as an A/B (able-bodied seaman). I was to stand the 8:00 to 12:00 watch, and was assigned a cabin by the generator room. The captain seemed to be only about forty years old, which was pretty young I thought at the time. But he seemed pleasant enough, then I went below to my cabin to store my belongings.

Since we were in port for a crew change and also to bring aboard supplies, I could see what the other crewmembers were up to. There was the normal compliment of deck personnel and engineers, but they also had technicians coming aboard who operated the equipment listening for any Soviet submarines. A couple of them were very obese, so I assumed that meant the food aboard must be good. But I also saw them bringing on many boxes themselves, maybe that was all entertainment material?

When I went up to the bridge, the first thing I noticed were the hand-railings everywhere coming out from the overhead, and it was from one side of the bridge to the other. *Uh oh.* That meant this thing must roll pretty heavily, surely I'd be finding out soon enough.

After everyone was aboard and we had everything loaded, we departed and set out to sea, heading around the island towards the north. Way off in the distance there was something out there, and as we got closer to being twelve nautical miles offshore from Oahu, it seemed to be waiting for us. Then I noticed what it was, a Soviet ship!

She came alongside us and stayed close to our starboard beam for two days straight, following our every move. Whenever a crewmember of our ship went out on deck, someone on the Soviet ship would snap their photograph. And that Soviet ship was a rust bucket like I'd never seen before. There was barely any visible paint anywhere on a surface, she was entirely rusted out, with scupper marks of suds down her sides as the only other coating on the hull.

And yes, our TAGOS ship did float like a cork, no wonder the hand-railings were everywhere. It was a good thing I'd taken a Dramamine before leaving port, or else I'd be heaving over the side by now, just like the poor wiper in the engine room was doing down in the bilges. He was never able to get used to the seas and the way this ship rolled, even throughout the entire voyage. At least he was able to hold food down after a while with medication, yet once we started listening for submarines, there was no stopping or going back.

After a few days the Soviet ship eventually left us, I imagine they'd followed this ship enough times to know when and where the surveying took place. This array used for listening was deployed once we got to the survey area, and it took over an hour to unroll the whole length of it from a long reel that led out over the stern. The technicians below were the ones who made all the decisions about what was done and when, so I just followed orders and assisted things as needed.

The rumor was that the array deployed in the water cost millions of dollars, especially when you included the cost of the special cable it was connected to. This was filled with some type of flammable liquid, and there was fire-fighting equipment situated all around the reel that housed it in case there was a fire or other accident. One of our drills was to man the foam nozzle for smothering any type of liquid fire, and another was to man the fire hoses to try and cool any flames before they melted surfaces in the area.

Since I was on the 8:00 to 12:00 watch, that meant I was with the third mate for this voyage. During the day, only one A/B would stand a watch on the bridge, and it was the same way at night. They had a chair in the corner that was suppose to be the captain's chair, but the third mate often sat in it. Since we were towing an array behind us, we were unable to maneuver as far as vessel traffic was concerned, so we had the right-of-way over any other vessels we might encounter.

This made the bridge watches fairly bland, as we sailed at a very slow speed and got all orders from the technicians on courses and speeds. They were situated in a locked control room a couple of decks below us, and I never entered that area as they had a special access key to get in and out that was needed. They were very careful to never talk about their jobs or what they listened for, or even how well the array was working. Once they placed us on a course and speed, we always stayed on it no matter if the ship rolled heavily or not.

And sometimes we hit heavy seas that rolled us substantially, to the point where the ship let out large groaning sounds. It was like the metal pieces flexing under stress let out warnings to us, with the worst point including skidding noises before a roll bottomed out. Sometimes it was bad enough to think we might do a complete flip underwater. On one night in particular, we had it the worst, and I ended up folding my mattress into a V-shape to somehow wedge myself inside of it—this was meant to keep me from falling out with the motion of the ship. The problem was every tenth roll or so there would be a much stronger roll that almost seemed to go too far—and would instantly wake me up, so for the entire night I ended up with only fifteen minutes of actual sleep.

While the food on the ship was good for the first week and a half just like they had described in the brochure, slowly we ran out of having fresh produce aboard, which left us with eating only what was frozen or canned. That wasn't bad when it came to lunch or dinner, but for breakfast they hadn't loaded any frozen food for us to eat. Instead, we had only eggs and bacon to last until the next time we hit port, and nobody knew when that might happen.

Unfortunately the steward, who was in charge of breakfast in the morning, wasn't helping things when it came to planning meals. Once a week she'd crack about 150 eggs into a big pot and scramble them together, then place it all inside the refrigerator. Whenever someone ordered scrambled eggs in the morning, she'd simply take this large ladle and spoon out some eggs from the pot and pour it into a pan, then scramble it over the stove.

During the first week the eggs were still yellow, but after the second week they were already getting a green tinge to them. Then by the third week it was scrambled green eggs all the way through, or even a green omelet could be ordered. But that wasn't all. She'd also cooked up a week's worth of bacon to go along with it at the same time, so only on the first day would we get freshly cooked bacon. By the end of the week it was hard and dried out with a refrigerator taste to it, and that's what she served us along with the green eggs.

The captain wasn't eager to do anything about this, I also found out that all of those boxes the technicians had brought aboard weren't full of entertainment items, many of them were boxes full of food and cooking supplies. That's why I wasn't seeing them having breakfast with us in the morning, instead they were eating what they'd brought aboard for themselves, and what they had simmering in their crock pots all day long.

There was one technician in particular who cooked more than the steward herself. She always had a crock pot boiling away that everyone could smell when walking by her cabin, and I bet it was twenty-times better than what we were being served. This technician was very plump and heavy, requiring a lot of food to hold her weight for a three month voyage. I wish she'd been the steward instead, but I never said that to anyone else or who knows what I'd be eating.

For those of us who were out at sea during our birthday, they had the steward ask us what kind of birthday cake we wanted. Since she hadn't baked a single decent thing so far all trip, when my birthday happened to come up, I wanted nothing more than one of the frozen Boston Cream Pies that we got every now and then that were halfway decent. I knew she couldn't screw-up one of those while unboxing it, and luckily I was right.

One thing about this ship being only 224 feet long was it could seem extra small if you had any problems with other crewmembers. I'd gotten along with almost everyone aboard the ship, but early on one of the engineers would make a comment about me whenever I was around him. And since it had already happened a couple of times, and then it happened once again, I thought of how to handle this—but one thing I couldn't do was go run to the captain, the bosun, or even the chief engineer about it. That would be the worst thing to do, having to tell someone else to tell this guy to stop ribbing me. Once that happens, then other crewmembers might join in, and I'd end up being worse off than before. And not only that, but I'd lose their respect. At least that's how I felt about it, and it seemed logical. You give a bully an inch, and they take a mile.

I had to do someone about it myself, I thought, and so the next time it happened, I was with another A/B in the passageway when this engineer showed up with another engineer. We talked and then he said something about me again. This time I asked him why every time we're around each other, he's got to be a smart ass and say something about me, and then I said it was going to stop —one way or the other. I told him if it happened again, then we were going to have to go at it, unless he wanted to go at it right now.

And then I gave him a look like I wanted to fight him. So what did he do? He backed down and said he was sorry, he didn't know it was bothering me. So that was that, he never said another thing to me for the rest of the trip, and it's not like it was my fault.

We stayed out at sea for quite a long time towing the array, it was a month and a half before we made it back into the Hawaiian port of Hilo. On the way in it was easy to spot the big island due to the volcanic ash in the air, there were fresh eruptions occurring at the Kilauea volcano. Since we had been out to sea for so long, the couple of other ships I'd been on had loaded fresh supplies for the crew to eat whenever we hit port. But what did our steward load?

I was shocked to find out she'd gone ashore with only forty dollars and bought enough fresh vegetables to last barely two days. That was it. For this crew of twenty-five people it was back to green eggs in short order, and she hadn't even bought any fresh eggs either! No wonder they had such a tough time finding crews, not only was the pay very low—but the food was even cheaper than the pay.

Once we got back out to sea, we headed north again, but this time we veered off later to head into a different area than before. The young captain knew this area well, as he told us to keep an eye out for glass balls that would be floating on the ocean. Apparently the ancient Japanese had used glass balls for floating their fishing nets for hundreds of years earlier, and those glass balls they'd lost ended up in this part of the Pacific Ocean floating around in circles forever.

But it wasn't only the glass balls seen floating, it seemed to be all of the garbage that was thrown over the side by every ship for the last hundred years as well. It was all circling out in this part of the ocean, like some gigantic wheel that went on spinning around forever. You could see endless pieces of plastic in all shapes and sizes, along with assorted bottles and Styrofoam pieces floating everywhere. We would watch it all as we slowly sailed by while towing the array behind the ship.

Eventually during the next day we saw one, it was a large glass ball floating amongst all the circling junk in the ocean. The captain was called to come out on deck, where he directed us to lower the inflatable lifeboat. And this was happening while we were still towing the array, so if we had an accident while launching or retrieving the inflatable, there was no way to save us. They couldn't stop the ship or else the array would sink and snap off—which meant the trip would end and probably the captain loses his job.

Fortunately we got the lifeboat launched safely, I rode aboard it with the second mate steering, and another A/B along with us. We sped back through the swells to retrieve the glass ball, and after we'd fishing it out of the ocean, the ship was already a mile behind and heading farther away from us. And boy, did she look small compared to that big ocean around us! If our lifeboat engine suddenly died out here, what could we do? They couldn't turn around and come get us, that was for sure.

We sped back to catch up to the ship, until we heard the captain yelling if we'd gotten the glass ball. After we proudly showed it to him, I climbed up the pilot ladder they'd hung over the side of the ship, along with the other A/B trailing behind me, while the second mate attached a hook onto the cradle to raise the inflatable lifeboat. We made it out and secured the inflatable without a hitch, and the captain was happy he got his glass ball. It was probably about fourteen inches across and it looked like it was very old indeed, and quite beautifully colored.

Besides knowing the quirks in the areas like this, the captain was an interesting guy to talk with. When we were on watch, we sometimes talked about our past lives, and that included chatting with the captain, who always seemed to have a story to tell. No matter what we'd done in our lives, though, the captain always had something that would beat us, and it was every time like that whenever we talked.

One time while on watch without the captain present, we talked about this, and we added up all the stories the captain had told us so far. He had five years living here, and seven years living there. Then twelve years doing this, and eight years doing that. We kept adding them up, until they got to be over sixty years worth of stories! But if the captain was only forty years old, that meant either he had a horrible memory, or he was one of the worst liars to ever sail aboard a ship—and it wasn't hard to figure out which of the two it was.

As promised, we had weekly drills aboard the ship, and some of them were for training or procedural type drills. During one time we had a fire drill at sea, we were towing the array behind the ship, and as usual, we were way out in the middle of nowhere. The captain told us he wanted to have a realistic drill this time, and we were to react as though the array was being retrieved and a fire broke out. This meant that we'd be applying foam to smother the fire, so we had someone at the foam monitor, and another A/B was below near the stern, with someone else on the other side by the shutoff valves, and I was at the upper fire station.

When the captain came out of the bridge and looked back, he yelled down to us that we were all dead because someone forgot to do something. Then he told us all to lay down on deck like we're dead. That's right, lay down and act like we're all dead! So there we were—in the middle of nowhere—flat on our backs while looking up at the blue sky above us and not moving. And yes, he even yelled at us not to move, for what seemed like ten minutes, just so he could think he was teaching us a lesson. The only thing we learned was that he was crazy, as nobody else would do that to us.

At the last port visit a couple of U.S. Navy cadets had come aboard to study the ship and learn our routines. They were both female, and the younger one was a redhead who fell for the third mate within a week or two at sea. Sometimes after he got off watch at midnight she would stay with him, and it quickly got around the ship what was happening. I think the captain came to resent her for doing this, but that wouldn't become a problem for another month, not until it came time for him to send in an evaluation of the two cadets.

We did get a new chief mate when we hit the next port, he was much older than everyone else aboard, and said he was a retired captain coming here as chief mate just for one trip—until he could learn the ropes as they say. He was very friendly and told me I could ask him any questions I wanted, and he'd even try to get me some time as a third mate aboard the ship. This time the steward didn't buy any fresh food when she went ashore, not even forty dollars worth. It was amazing how cheap this outfit was, but there was nothing we could do about it. I only had another month left to go on this ship, as I'd promised them three months for this trip and then three months of vacation at home, to return as a third mate for the following voyage.

I was still standing watches with the same third mate, who'd mentioned he knew a famous pitcher with the Atlanta Braves at one time. He was out here to get enough sea time to upgrade his license, and for a third mate, that meant one year at sea to sit for his second mate's license. Then a year as second mate to sit for his chief mate's license. But there was little else to talk about and after a while, it became a monotonous trip. Since our TAGOS vessel floated like a cork on the ocean, we floated with it and were eventually put into a dreamy state at night unless the rolling was too severe.

This especially happened as we sailed in and out through the doldrums where there were no other ships sighted for days and weeks. Besides the Soviet ships that occasionally tailed us, it was nothing but the ocean and our ship rocking us all day long like we were in a baby's cradle. On the night watches there was little maneuvering, perhaps the technician's might call up and give a slight bump up or down in speed for the array, or maybe ask for a tiny course change, but it was like that every night it seemed. And sometimes the third mate was in that comfy captain's chair, did I even see him nod off every now and then? No, it couldn't be, but I wouldn't have said anything even if he did.

Sometimes I'd go and check on things inside the engine room out of curiosity during the day, just to see the equipment they used and how well it ran. The engineers kept the place very clean, with everything operating and looking to be in perfect working order. That's what I thought of the area anyways, until on one occasion I was told one of the secrets in the engine room. An engineer was there and pointed to an elbow fitting that entered the hull. He said it was the main intake for the seawater to cool the engines, and when they built the ship, they'd installed an intake elbow made of a different metal other than steel.

He said since the hull and the piping around it were all steel, this was causing a galvanic corrosion to this fitting as the seawater passed through it. And since it was located below the waterline, there was no way to repair it safely while at sea. He also said they'd covered this fitting with epoxy to try and keep it from splitting open, but if by chance that epoxy didn't hold, the ship could flood and sink within ten minutes, assuming a total breakup of the part. *Was he kidding?* I didn't think so, as the fitting looked awfully weak to me, but it never leaked and I checked it every so often for the remainder of the trip just to be sure.

While aboard I sometimes talked with the second mate, but not often, at least as far as lengthy conversations went. He was on the 12:00 to 4:00 watch and would relieve us with his A/B, but sometimes we'd chat while eating together in the galley at dinner. One time in particular it was about him being the medical officer aboard ship. If any crewmembers fell ill at sea and needed any medications like aspirin or Pepto-Bismol, they would see him about it.

It just so happened that he was very giddy to tell us what he'd experienced. One of the female navy cadets came to him with a medical issue and wanted his opinion about it. He didn't say exactly what it was, only that she had undressed and he'd given her a medical exam. That included looking at her private parts along with the rest of her. He didn't mention what she had or what the prognosis might be, but was happy that he'd performed the task as the medical officer. And then he kept on smiling away as he ate the rest of his meal with us.

We eventually came back into port and docked at Pearl Harbor again, and since my three months was nearly over, I decided to go to the airport and rent a car. I hadn't really seen much of the island so far, only the taxi ride to and from the air base and other than that—not much else. Word quickly got around that I had rented a car, and there was another A/B aboard who'd signed on earlier a few weeks back. He was an interesting character because he was missing his top front teeth and he'd never had them replaced. He also had been acting like a perfect angel ever since he came aboard, never swearing or even showing any signs of aggression. I had a strange feeling about him though, like he was hiding a secret and was fresh out of prison, as that's usually where they knock out the front teeth of inmates. The reason for that I won't say, but it isn't pleasant.

When this new A/B found out I had rented a car, he told me I should let him borrow it since we were both buddies, and good buddies aboard a ship have to share and share alike. He wanted to give me a guilt complex over it, or so he tried. Since at the time he was standing a watch, I agreed to think about it until later.

Eventually I went back to him, knowing I had to get out of this somehow. That's when I explained about the rental agreement not insuring him as a driver. Too bad, I told him, but he couldn't use the rental car. He then acted like it was no big deal, and I was happy to have gotten out of it.

Later I took the rental car out for a drive, and one of the places I wanted to see was the famous Hotel Street in Honolulu. Another crewmember had told me how all of the sailors in Pearl Harbor had walked along it during World War II while looking for female companionship. There were so many sailors going, they would line up and wait for hours outside of the brothels to get in. But when I drove out, Hotel Street was now a one-way street that only busses used, and I didn't know that. Not seeing any signs against it, I turned down and started to drive along Hotel Street, when a cop was right there to stop me. He asked me what I was doing, so I told him I was lost and heading back to Hickam Air Force Base. He kindly let me go after giving me directions. From there I went up the coast, and spent as much time away from the ship as possible, only returning when my next watch came up later in the evening.

The new chief mate had quickly worked it so I could get some watch time as a third mate aboard the ship. The regular third mate had left to go home, so I was briefly promoted to stand his gangway watches while in port. It just so happened that on my next watch as third mate from 8:00 p.m. to midnight, the A/B who'd wanted to use my rental car showed up very late that night on the dock, while behaving very drunk and disorderly.

This experience reminded me of my cadet friend back in Cabo San Lucas—the one who'd drank the tequila, but this A/B coming back was much worse. He wasn't just threatening everyone he saw aboard with fists, he started to threaten us with something even more dangerous. He'd brought a gun to the ship and had given it to the captain for safekeeping while we were at sea. Now he demanded his gun back and was telling each of us from the dock how much he hated everyone. He was also accusing us of things that weren't true, saying he could read our minds about what we were thinking.

There's an old theory that alcohol brings out the real person from within after enough drinks are consumed. It's sort of like if one is a lover at heart, then they become a Don Juan after a few beers. But if a person is a criminal at heart, then they turn into an Al Capone. And this guy while drunk was acting like a thug to the crew he'd just been working with and hadn't said much to while sober. But now he had everything to say, and it was all the alcohol talking. Even worse, had I let him use my rental car that night, he'd probably have crashed it pretty quickly. I had dodged a bullet in more ways than one.

After the captain arrived at the gangway, the A/B was told he wasn't allowed back on the ship, since his screaming was reaching the nearby Navy docks. It wasn't hard to hear him yelling in the clear night air, so he finally left and stayed off the ship until the next day—once he'd sobered up. Then he was let aboard again and the captain signed him off as a crewmember. He took everything, including his gun—but without the bullets—and he left Hawaii, off to somewhere else that nobody cared to know about.

Another crewmember that seemed to be having a hard time of it was the new chief mate, who had come aboard after retiring as a captain. He'd been very happy when he first met us, but slowly the trip wore on him. Perhaps part of it was because I'd been annoying him with too many questions, and he barked at me once when he returned from being ashore. I also thought the chief mate was under pressure from the captain on how he was supposed to handle his duties. The captain was acting like our ship was a complex calculus equation, when it really was more like simple arithmetic instead. There were no cargo operations, we had a small crew, plus we barely hit ports. Could it get any easier than that? I wondered. And all of the course and speed changes came from the technicians when we were towing, instead of from the actual officers on watch.

The two U.S. Navy cadets also left the ship while in port, allowing the captain to forward his evaluation of them. I don't know what he was thinking, but we eventually found out the captain gave a bad assessment on the redhead cadet. This was sent to the Navy brass and they weren't very happy after reading it. Quickly they fired the captain, just as I was preparing to leave after my three months of sea time were up. At times during the trip I thought the captain had acted crazy, but still I never guessed they would do this, no matter how much he thought of himself. But apparently he'd done something that a civilian captain wasn't allowed to do, namely run down the U.S. Navy. It was the straw that broke the camel's back, and he was gone.

Also leaving at the same time was another A/B from the cabin next to mine, he had wanted to sail for only three months, and they promised him he could leave after that. He packed up all his belongings and went off to the company's main office, assuming he was to leave the ship for good. But then he returned. "They won't let me leave," he told me at the gangway. "They threatened to keep my papers and call the Coast Guard to report me. If I don't do what they say, it may take nine months to get my papers back, but they promised if I stay aboard for another three months, then they'll let me sign off. I agreed—so am staying for another run."

Ha ha, I thought. Shanghaied by the company.

For some reason this A/B had started to dislike me after I'd told a harmless joke he didn't find very funny. That occurred about half-way through the trip, and ever since then he'd given me the cold shoulder when I saw him. Now he was stuck for at least three more months on the ship.

Fortunately I had promised the company that I'd come back as a third mate after my upcoming vacation time was over, and they believed me. The captain then signed me off for good and gave me all of my sailing papers. I was careful in not talking about my plans with him, however, as I had no intention of returning to sail with TAGOS ever again. Not that it wasn't a good operation to get some sea time and experience, but the pay was so low I barely ended up with a few thousand dollars for three months at sea. Yet I had to keep my options open, so I left on good terms with everyone, and then flew home from Honolulu.

Believe it or not, when I got back home and opened up my luggage, that's when I noticed a few things had been stolen. It wasn't much in terms of valuables—only an old Sony Walkman and a couple of other things like a battery pack and a charger, nothing to get too worked up about. But then I tried to think of where these things could've been stolen, and came up with it either being the airport workers or the A/B that got stuck doing the extra three months on the ship.

The cabins that we stayed in aboard the TAGOS ship shared a single bathroom between adjacent ones. When we went in to use it, there was a lock on the other door to keep out the other crewmember. There was also a lock on the door to enter the bathroom from the outside, so a crewmember couldn't enter our cabin when we weren't there. Perhaps I'd forgot to lock it, and he came in and took some of my things? I imagined if he did then he thought he was pretty smart—but I was at home and he was still stuck on the ship for another three months. I still had the last laugh after all, no matter what.

6

Headed For Karachi

Only two months after returning home, I'd already found my next job! By chance there was an ad looking for A/B's placed at the academy, and when I called the company's agent, he told me of an opening in the Persian Gulf. He mentioned it was a dangerous job since the supertanker was loading in Kuwait, and that meant Iraqi soldiers were occasionally shooting at the ship. He said something about barriers being erected to stop any bullets, then said he would get me out on the ship in a couple of weeks if I wanted it.

After a week passed, the agent called me up and told me of a change in plans. The supertanker in the Persian Gulf was definitely out of the question, instead he wanted me on another supertanker that was going to load grain for Karachi. She was docked in Oregon, and he wanted me out there as soon as possible. The job sounded very interesting, so I agreed and got everything I needed for the trip ready, then headed out to the airport. This flight was happening during one of the strongest November storms we'd had in years, but the takeoff went fine, and so was the trip out along the coast.

But when the airplane tried landing at the Portland airport, it seemed like we were being twisted by a tornado. The airplane hit the runway hard and bounced, then hit hard and bounced again and again—as the brakes tried grabbing each time we briefly touched down. This was the roughest landing I'd ever felt! We were being pushed to the side as the plane was angled by the wind, and I finally gave a sigh of relief when the tires stayed down and started to brake. That was scary!

After I got off the plane, an A/B waiting at the arrival gate introduced himself as a member of the crew. He was there to take me to the ship, which was moored on the other side of Portland, down along the Willamette River docks.

We got my bags and headed out, getting onto the freeway and heading in the direction of the downtown area. After a short while later, up ahead there was a large bridge that crossed the river. Since it was still storming outside, once we reached half-way across it, we could really see the effects of the wind on the river below us. Then the A/B pointed out our ship, noticing she'd broken away in the storm. We could see her stern well off the dock, and crewmembers frantically trying to winch her back in.

That's where we were headed, down to this supertanker that was the largest in the U.S. fleet. At 1,120 feet long, with a beam (width) of 178 feet, she was even larger than an aircraft carrier. Since the oil market was so weak at the time, the ship's owner had decided to convert her into a grain carrier, where after being fully-loaded she'd take her cargo of wheat to India—where it would feed millions of people.

By the time we got down to the dock, the crew had successfully got the ship winched back alongside it, then we waited as the gangway was set down so we could get aboard. I couldn't believe the size of this ship! At the dock all I saw looking back was a steel wall that was over sixty feet above my head. And when I got up the gangway, her bow and stern were both over 500 feet away in either direction. The main deck had open oil barrels placed in large bunches at various spots all along the deck. They weren't located in any conceivable pattern, more like they were placed in any available spot and left there—to be filled with oily sludge from the tanks below. And there were hundreds and hundreds of these barrels scattered around everywhere, going out in all directions.

Then I noticed the open deck plates that were large enough to fall through. These were normally around the ship to allow for air blowers to blast fresh air down into the tanks to clear the atmosphere out, and also used to hang rubber hoses with nozzles for cleaning and washing the tanks themselves. It took a special wrench to remove the cover to one of these openings, but the covers were also left on the deck nearby, waiting to be tripped over if one wasn't careful. Next I noticed the cargo pipes crossing the decks, and the steel mooring cables stretched across the main deck from the winches. If someone wasn't careful, they might walk into one and cut their shin or even worse, trip over one and land on their face. Wow, this place was dangerous!

I went towards the stern of the ship and climbed up to the next deck, then entered the house and found my way up to the captain's office. That was the first thing I learned to do after boarding any ship, as he needed to sign me on as a crewmember first— where he checked my paperwork and saw that I'm fit to work. After I greeted the captain in his office, he signed me on as an A/B and told me I was under the direct supervision of the bosun. Below I was shown my cabin and where to place my belongings.

Since it was just after lunch, the deck gang was going out to work again after having retrieved the ship earlier in the storm and eaten a quick meal. I stayed behind momentarily and changed into my grungiest clothes to fit in with the rest of the deck crew. I definitely didn't want to go out on deck in my newest clothes and stick out like a sore thumb on my first day. After about twenty minutes, the bosun showed up at my cabin and was angry with me. He'd walked all the way up forward to the bow, which on this ship was a long walk, and then had to come all the way back to get me. Since he was about sixty-five years old, that was a lot of effort, so he was pretty unhappy. He had snow white hair with a long beard, and wore a dark green raincoat everywhere he went since it was the rainy season. I apologized for not being faster, then the two of us went down onto the main deck and started walking up forward to work with the rest of the deckhands.

I learned they were still in the process of washing tanks, and whichever mate was on duty would direct the washing for that watch, as long as daylight lasted. During the day the chief mate was handling this, and so we'd do the manual work of moving rubber hoses around and dropping or raising them deep into the huge cargo tanks. These tanks were absolutely enormous in size, to lower a nozzle to the bottom might take about eighty feet of hose just from deck level. Then the chief mate would climb into the tank and show us where they had to be tied off, usually in an area that had evaded an earlier cleaning.

The manhole openings that were used to enter these tanks were large and led to steel ladders that wound down, back and forth, until they eventually made it to the bottom of the tanks. There was usually at least one blower above that used compressed air to run it. These directed fresh air down into the tanks as we worked below. Lights were also lowered so we could see where we were walking, although some sunlight shined in through every plate opening. As we walked down one of these ladders, we could feel the oily layers on each step, and they were very slippery. The handrails were also slippery, so between the two it was a chore to make it down very far without a first slip on a step—which also meant a frantic grab to keep from falling further. At the bottom of the tanks were rows of huge cargo pipes. These ran the entire length of the lower ship as they passed through each tank and made their way back into the pumproom.

The pumproom was at the stern end of the main cargo tanks for gravity reasons, so as the ship was normally unloaded, we wanted to keep the cargo in the back tanks for last to allow gravity to help with pumping the ship dry. The main cargo pumps were also at the very bottom of the pumproom, and the pumps on this ship were huge all by themselves. Each was larger than a small car, with a platform built around them so we could walk over and inspect them up close.

The third mate aboard had been on the ship for some time—he said it was a little over five months so far. As he talked about the ship, he reminded me of a young cowboy talking about a long cattle drive, where he was nearly at the end of their trail. They'd been cleaning tanks at the dock ever since the ship first arrived, and he seemed about ready to need a vacation.

Inside the control room where I met him were old newspapers, and some of them had articles written about the ship. One reported about a lawsuit involving the grain contract. It said the supertanker's prior owner had defaulted on some government-guaranteed loans, so the U.S. Maritime Administration, which had helped to finance the ship's construction, had taken over possession of her. Then the current owner purchased the ship from the U.S. Maritime Administration for $7.1 million, which was barely over scrap value. Next the owner won a massive grain contract that was reserved for U.S. flag vessels only, and $9.3 million was the winning bid. It mentioned a lawsuit was filed by two bulk carriers who'd lost out on the bidding, along with two maritime unions who intended to block the ship from fulfilling its government-sponsored relief contract. This was all still being litigated, and it seemed very confusing to understand it all.

As I sat there reading this, the third mate told me about some of the other crewmembers we had working on the ship, pointing out that we had a couple of females aboard who did cleaning in both the licensed crew quarters and the galley. One was technically the bosun's girlfriend, and the other was a much younger brunette who was an ex-heroine addict taking methadone from a local clinic to stay clean. He said they normally hung around with the crew when they weren't working, and even would come into the berthing areas after work.

Most nights, as I quickly found out, that meant a lot of drinking aboard, with constant alcohol being served by the A/B's, who acted and drank like prohibition was coming. If there was a record for drinking booze aboard U.S. ships, these guys might've tied it. One of them was also a horse-racing addict besides being an alcoholic, and he'd stay up all night on weekends doing calculations about the next day's races at the local race track. I asked him how he did one time and he said it went well, so he must've been good at it.

The chief steward in the galley was the greatest chef I'd ever seen, he was a cooking addict and it showed. He was always preparing something in there all day long, and even at times when I got up early, he was there baking cookies or cakes. If anyone was hungry, he'd even make something out of scratch for us, and it always tasted great. I'd been gaining weight ever since arriving thanks to him, and it was nearly all muscle. That was due to working on deck and constantly pulling hoses, pushing around blowers and moving around other equipment for the tank cleaning. It was like going to a gym for eight hours a day and being paid to do it. Then he'd serve us amazing food, including steaks and roasts. We couldn't help but get in shape under those circumstances. And when the ship's owner came aboard wearing what looked like a five thousand dollar suit one day, he was treated like royalty as well. The steward made him the best food, it was the one area where they never scrimped on the costs.

Shortly after arriving, some of the barrels filled with oily sludge aboard were starting to be removed from the main deck by the crew running a crane. These were lifted up, one by one, and swung over the side, where they were dropped into an empty dumpster positioned on the dock. I couldn't believe it when I saw what was happening since the dumpster had no liner, allowing the dropped barrels to spill their oily contents and slowly drain out, with some of it ending up down in the river. It was strange how no visitors noticed any of this when they came aboard the ship, but the workers quickly paused this operation for obvious reasons.

Also during the day, they started to bring extra workers aboard to help us after the ship's owner had hired another tank cleaning crew. They were meant to assist us in getting things ready for loading the grain, this was especially important after an official tank inspection had failed, so now they hurried everyone to get the ship cleaned up on time. The grain contract stated the ship was to be ready before the end of the month for loading, and that deadline was quickly approaching.

Every morning a couple of buses began arriving by the dock with outside workers to help us clean the tanks. These happened to be people from the local homeless shelter that they'd hired for very low wages, and they directed them to come aboard and do the dangerous task of entering the tanks to help with scraping the oil and cleaning the residue. But since the ship was so large, there were many places to hide everywhere—either amongst the many tanks, or even up forward in the focsle area.

I learned not to go up forward after finding many used hypodermic needles being left behind, with some bloody rags being discarded along with them. However this ship wasn't the place to be shooting up drugs and then trying to walk along the oily pipes down inside the deep tanks. Shortly after these workers started helping us, we began to get slips and falls from them stumbling on the cargo pipes.

The large crane on the dock could cover the whole area around the ship and was used to assist in moving barrels full of oily residue around or to direct equipment up and down through the open manholes on top of the tanks. At first when one of the workers slipped at the bottom of a tank and injured himself, we called the paramedics and placed the worker in one of our stretchers, then had the crane hook onto that to raise him out.

When the paramedics came aboard the ship, they were told where the hurt worker was located, and walked over to the open manhole on deck above him. They wouldn't get closer than five feet to the opening though, and had facial expressions as though they were looking down into hell itself. The thought of falling through that hole to a tank bottom over eighty feet down was a frightening thought, and after I saw their reaction, I realized we were so used to standing next to the openings that maybe we were all crazy for even working here.

Once the crane started to raise the hurt worker out of the tank, you could see he was frightened as he looked up towards the small opening above him. And the closer he got to the top of the tank, the more frightened he seemed to get. Then came the scariest part, he had to be tipped up to get him through the narrow opening. Sheer panic took over as he imagined himself slipping out through the bottom of the stretcher and falling all the way down to his death. Luckily, that didn't happen—he came up safely and the paramedics took him away.

After he was gone and they began working in the same tank again, one of the remaining workers decided to demonstrate how the first one had hurt himself. He climbed up on a huge oil pipe at the bottom of the tank and proceeded to slip off it, then hit himself on the back of the head just like the first worker did. Now we had to rescue him as well, so the paramedics were called out a second time. Over the course of the next few days, there were even more workers that were taken out of tanks from falling, but each time the paramedics never returned our stretchers from a previous visit. So by the fifth injury, we had to wait until they came aboard and then went back to retrieve a stretcher, which delayed us even further.

Suddenly the tank cleaning company got fired when they failed to have the required insurance to cover the growing number of injured workers. It seemed a little late to be worried over this, but for now we were back to doing all the tank cleaning ourselves until the next company was hired. And that happened very quickly, with the new company picking up where the last one had left off—by bringing in many outside workers.

Next I was put on the gangway watch after it was broken by rolling along the dock into a steel bollard. It was strange because the ship went up and down against the dock like there was a large tide occurring on the Willamette River, causing the gangway landing to constantly roll. However the ship was nearly empty and over seventy feet out of the water, so when you subtracted the height of the dock, that meant walking sixty feet up the gangway alongside the steel hull plates—and by the time you hit the main deck, you'd felt every foot of them.

The gangway platform was lifted up and down by an electric winch that had a controller connected to it. One button made it lift up, the other button made it drop down—it couldn't be any easier. So I stood my seven-day watch from midnight to 8:00 a.m. and kept adjusting the gangway every hour until the day crew came out in the morning to relieve me, then I'd be allowed to go hit the bunk. One odd thing was at night I had to mostly lower the gangway during the seven days I attended it, with the ship slowly lifting higher out the water each night. I'd later learn why that was happening, but for now I thought it had to be due to some crazy tides in the area. Also, a new second mate came aboard, replacing the old one leaving after a long stay with the ship.

Eventually my week of doing the gangway watch was over, so I went back to day work with the other A/B's and the bosun. They told me about more workers being injured from falling in the tanks, and each time the paramedics never returned any of our stretchers.

There was one other casualty to report, and it occurred after they'd hired an inert gas generator to be used. It was nothing more than a diesel engine on a barge and had been tied off on the starboard fantail. While it was running, one of the workers responsible decided he needed to pull a fuse, and attempted to do it without shutting off the engine. When I first saw him, his hand was quickly swelling up, but he kept telling everyone he wasn't hurt. The metal watch around his wrist looked like it was melted, he must have touched too close to the terminals when pulling out the fuse. Off on a stretcher he went, making it nine casualties before we'd even loaded any cargo aboard.

Another oddity was we kept washing the tanks with the oily wash-water having to end up somewhere after we finished each day, but by the next morning all the tanks were dry. A mate was seemingly up all night moving water around and getting the ship ready for the next day's cleaning. It just so happened that when I went out onto the dock before we started work one morning, I couldn't believe it, there was oil in the river between the ship and the shoreline. The fumes were fairly pungent, if anyone had thrown a lit match, the oil would've starting burning on the surface of the river.

When I went back aboard, other people nearby had already seen the oil, including other workers. One of the A/B's even brought it up later that morning, and when we checked again, all of the oil was gone. I'd forgotten about this until the captain called me into his office a couple of days later and said the third mate was leaving the ship as his time was up. Then he asked me if I wanted his job, and suddenly I remembered that oil in the river.

I asked him if I could think about it for five minutes, and he seemed puzzled but said yes. Then I walked out into the passageway and tried to decide what to do. If I told him no, that meant they'd bring in another third mate and I'd be stuck sailing as an A/B for a few more months. But if I said yes—and they asked me to do cargo operations that might put oil in the river—I could lose my license. It was a big decision to make and after thinking it over, I went back to see the captain.

After finding the captain I told him I'd take the job. He asked me if I meant the third mate's job, so I said yes, but only under one condition—"I won't be spilling any oil."

He said he didn't want a third mate worried about crapping his pants.

"I won't be doing that, Captain, but I also won't be spilling any oil."

I was surprised when he said OK, and then he signed me on as the new third mate.

Wow, I was the new third mate on the largest supertanker in the U.S. fleet, and it's being converted into a grain carrier. Who'd have ever thunk it. Unfortunately, I didn't have much time to enjoy things, as on my second watch the U.S. Coast Guard came aboard and halted all our operations. They'd been tipped off to the earlier oil spill by a phone call reporting it.

They ordered us to cease moving around all oil and wash-water within the ship, but would allow the tank cleaning to continue. They also brought in every crewmember to interview about what had caused the 5,000 gallon oil spill, and wanted to know who was responsible. When my turn came, I simply told them I'd been promoted the day earlier to third mate and the oil spill happened before me, and I'd never touched any of the cargo controls.

That must've worked, because they allowed me to stay on as a crewmember, but they removed the captain, the chief mate, and the second mate. Suddenly, I was the only licensed deck officer aboard!

For one day I was the big shot, the bosun even came up as I walked down the main deck and asked me what to do concerning the deck plates and a couple of other things, so I told him what seemed best. It wasn't anything earth-shattering to decide about, we were all still kind of shocked over what the Coast Guard had done the day before.

The following day a new captain showed up, along with a fresh chief mate. The captain didn't say much, but it was rumored amongst the crew that he'd come out of retirement for this job after being fired from one of the large oil companies a few years earlier. He seemed friendly enough to me, he was certainly of retirement age, or thereabouts.

Later that afternoon the captain came to me and said he hated to do this for a first assignment, but someone had stolen a wallet from one of the A/B's, and he wanted me to frisk all the tank cleaners we had aboard. There were about fifty of them, and they were scattered in different tanks, all wearing rain gear and jackets in this wintry weather. I thought how could I frisk fifty people and expect to find such a small wallet on this massive ship? Was he serious?

"Yes" was the reply when I asked if he's sure, so I went and found the bosun, then told him we had to frisk all of the tank cleaners. Get them rounded up aft and we'll try to find the missing wallet. At this time the main cargo deck on the ship was still covered with open oil barrels everywhere, mostly full of oily residue and filling up even further with rain water. It was around a group of these barrels that we started to frisk them.

The tank cleaners lined up, and then, one by one, they emptied their pockets as I pretended to check that they had nothing else. We did this until all of them had been frisked, and you guessed it, we found nothing. Then the wallet was found floating in one of the nearby open oil barrels, so we got it back after all. What a miracle! The money in the wallet was missing, but at least it was found. I gave out a big sigh of relief.

The next night a new second mate came aboard, and we briefly met before he disappeared to head off into the berthing area. I found out the following day that he'd slipped a note under the chief mate's door in the middle of the night saying he wasn't staying, and had left the ship. Were things really that bad here?

The chief steward at this time also decided to leave, but it wasn't because he had done anything wrong, or because the crew didn't like him. He had been aboard for almost six months and needed to get off. The crew begged him to stay, a couple even offered to pay him some extra money. He was the best steward any of us had ever seen, but he left as he said, and was replaced soon enough.

The new steward was unfortunately the complete opposite—he was exactly what everyone had feared. He wasn't up all day cooking like the last one, and never cooked anything at night. Gone were the extra meals, the perfectly sautéed steaks, fluffy omelets and roasted pork dishes. It was from feast to famine, and the crew became very unhappy. I even lost weight due to him arriving, as all the extra muscle I'd built up by pulling hoses or lowering nozzles everywhere was now withering away out of hunger.

They'd also sent us another second mate, and this one decided to stay aboard. Now we finally had all of our deck officers again, meanwhile the U.S. Coast Guard would begin allowing us to discharge wash-water to a barge that came alongside the ship during the day. This was all being done under their supervision, with a member of the Coast Guard constantly watching us and everything we did from now on.

One thing they also made sure of—we couldn't allow any rain water falling on the main deck to go over the side. This was solved by closing off all of the scupper holes with wooden plugs, which forced the rain water to collect back aft along both sides of the main house. There we placed pneumatic pumps at the collection points to suck the rain water up and discharge it into the large segregated ballast tank nearby. Since it was already dirty from earlier operations, the U.S. Coast Guard allowed this, with the understanding that the tank would be washed before our departure.

By the way, it was an amazing feat, but on my watch we only allowed the rain water to overflow once, and that was when the pumps froze up badly during a major downpour. A U.S. Coast Guard person was standing there watching when a tiny drop of oil went over the side with the rain water. He claimed we were spilling oil, yet it was only a tiny drop! I quickly got the pumps running again and it was the only time that happened, but technically I spilled a whole drop of oil, assuming it made it down the eighty feet of hull to the waterline.

Next, in order to start discharging the wash-water from tank cleaning to a barge, we used various reducers at the cargo manifold to downsize the discharge connection. Then a long, heavy hose was bolted there, with the other end being lowered over the side, where a worker on the barge connected it at his end. Since the main cargo pump on this line hadn't been started up recently, the second mate sent me down into the pumproom, where I was to listen and see if it ran smoothly during start-up.

So I took a walkie-talkie and headed towards the pumproom, then started down all the winding stairs, eventually going eighty feet down to the lowest catwalk that surrounded the pumps. I called the second mate and said I'm in position, so go ahead. All three cargo pumps I saw were massive in size, even larger than VW beetles, with huge cargo pipes connecting to them. Briefly, I waited a moment for something to happen, then one of the three pumps whirled as it slowly started. It began to sound OK, but suddenly the second mate ran it at full speed, and oh hell, it was sucking air. That made the pump start to scream, going much faster than it should've been, and it was racing like it wanted to explode.

Quickly I yelled into the walkie-talkie for the second mate to shut off the pump, but the sound in the pumproom was too loud for him to hear me. I instantly imagined the pump breaking apart now, with pieces flying everywhere, and me being splattered on the bulkheads in all directions. I thought I was about to die, right then and there.

With the cargo pump still screaming like a jet engine during take off, I started to run up the ladders, still yelling into the walkie-talkie to shut it down. No way could I hear back, but maybe he'd hear the sound of the pump! I kept running up, until I made it half-way up and took a deep breath as my heart pounded at two hundred beats a second. Then I continued up, and finally made it out alive. *Whew!* Below me I could still hear the pump screaming at full speed.

When I got into the control room out of breath, the second mate was over in a corner, and I asked him why he hadn't shut the pump off. He casually said he'd forgotten, and then walked over and turned it off. I couldn't believe it. I felt lucky to be alive, how that pump didn't break apart was a miracle. What a jerk for not paying attention, but what could I do? I sat down to catch my breath while he left—maybe he noticed me steaming mad.

In the control room, I saw on the table that the ship was still making the newspapers, with the latest article being about the difficulties in getting the tank cleaning finished. This coverage had caught the attention of a local elementary school, and as a result one morning I noticed a young kid looking around out on deck. I quickly went over and asked him how he'd gotten aboard, and was told his father had brought him. He said they were studying the ship in his classroom and he wanted to see our operations up close.

Then his father came over to talk, so I took them into the control room and off the main deck. I explained how dangerous it was out there, with all of the open deck plates around, someone so small could easily trip and fall through all the way to the bottom. But then the kid started to talk about the ship—how large she was, where she was built, and how long she'd been sitting here. He even knew how much grain she would carry, and how many tanks she had. He knew more than I did, maybe even more than the captain too. The father took some photographs of his son with the crew, and I showed them the bridge, then they promised to never come back. It was pure luck that nothing had happened to his wonderful young son.

Now the tank cleaning was progressing well, and at this point it was getting close to being finished. The barrels scattered all around the ship were being removed at a decent pace now. Maybe these were signs the ship might actually be ready soon for loading grain?

On something unrelated; the bosun, a few of the A/B's, and the two female workers went ashore together to be tested for the HIV virus, yet didn't talk much about why they needed it. I only assumed that since one of them had a history of needle use, there might be more than just drinking going on in the berthing areas at night. Luckily they all tested negative, but that slowed down some of their partying until they all finally got the news.

By chance the ship's owner came aboard again to get a progress report from the captain, and to eat some excellent food from the steward. He was still wearing what looked to be a five thousand dollar suit—I guess if he owned a seven million dollar ship, and could afford to load ten million dollars worth of cargo, a suit like that was mere pocket change to him. Then he learned what the crew had found out the hard way—the food was much worse now than when he was last aboard. The next day the steward was replaced, but it wasn't the last one coming back, instead it was a decent enough chef, but still not as good as the original.

Finally the day came when all of the cargo tanks were inspected and passed by the Grain Inspection Service. Even the segregated ballast tanks had been stripped, washed and cleaned, and were inspected by the U.S. Coast Guard. Now all we had left to do was clear the main deck of any oily residue, remove all the oil-soaked absorbent materials with the remaining barrels full of sludge, and then secure the cargo tanks for loading.

We were scheduled to shift to a different dock in Portland for the first load containing 73,000 metric tons of grain. From there they had us heading up to Tacoma, where we'd load another 87,000 metric tons more. Finally, we'd be topping off the ship in Seattle with the final 48,000 tons. That all added up to be 208,000 metric tons, which would be the largest single load of grain ever completed in the Pacific Northwest, breaking the old record of 160,000 metric tons by a substantial margin.

After the final inspections all passed, we were shifted to the grain dock in Portland. A pilot and four tugboats were used for the move, and considering all the problems we'd encountered earlier, to even start loading was a miracle in itself. But operations started smoothly, it was like they wanted us out of Portland as much as we wanted to get out. And that we did, once the scheduled amount of grain was placed into the tanks. To accomplish this, the long-shoremen maneuvered a grain chute over the ship's cargo deck using a handheld controller. Whichever cargo tanks were scheduled to be loaded with grain, they had their plate covers removed. Then the grain chute was centered over each of those openings and they commenced loading.

Meanwhile, in the control room I'd read another newspaper article brought aboard concerning our ship. It mentioned another lawsuit involving injury claims being filed by over a dozen of the tank cleaners, some of whom had been hauled out on stretchers.

It also said immigration officials were investigating the hiring of undocumented workers among them. None of this affected the grain loading though, and after getting the 73,000 metric tons aboard—we finally left Portland and all of those troubles behind— only to find new ones up in Tacoma.

We were scheduled to load 87,000 metric tons at the next grain dock, which we started at the end of December. But union members started picketing outside our ship because we were non-union workers—and it stopped our loading operations again. The company knew it had no choice but to agree to a union vote. That's when one interesting thing happened during my evening watch right after we started back up, with the captain being upset about it the next morning. He wondered why I hadn't logged the reason we only loaded grain for fifteen minutes the night before? I fixed that by putting this into the logbook:

LATE ENTRY:

2000 to 2315: Loading operations halted when longshoremen claimed unsafe working conditions after a single light bulb burned out on deck. Electrician called.

2315 to 2330: Commenced loading grain after light bulb replaced.

2330 to 2400: All work stopped for union coffee break.

The captain and chief mate were pleased—my new logbook entry showed almost four hours of cargo time wasted over a burned-out light bulb. Another time during loading I was called a scab by one of the longshoremen just because the ship was non-union. When his co-worker heard this, he told him to be quiet, as he knew we were to have a union vote on the ship before we sailed.

Eventually the port side of the ship was finished with loading the grain, so a pilot brought in five tugs to swing her around and place the starboard side against the dock to continue. This was done because the ship was so wide, the conveyor system couldn't reach all the way across her. And as this loading continued, it made maneuvering the ship more difficult due to the enormous weight of the cargo aboard. Just to bring her to the dock took the crew five hours, whereas a normal-sized ship would take two tugs about an hour to complete.

The loading on the starboard side went well, but there was one last maneuver to do before finishing at this dock. We had to move the ship forward and adjust the mooring cables so the last tank could be reached. When the time came, I went up on the bridge with the captain, while the deck gang either slacked out or reeled in the mooring cables with the deck winches. The captain used a walkie-talkie to give them orders and also gave me commands as I stood at the engine controls. It was either dead slow or stop in either direction to get the ship relocated.

It just so happened that a couple of people from a shipping company came by to talk with the captain just after we'd started, and one of them had been to the California Maritime Academy as a cadet. He recognized me up on the bridge and started asking me how I got this job, where did I apply, and whom did I call. He talked so much I couldn't hear the captain way out on the bridge-wing telling me to stop the engines. Fortunately nothing happened when I missed his order, but there wouldn't be another one. I told my new friend we'd talk after our maneuvering was finished, now please don't get me fired.

Then after the last tank was loaded in Tacoma, we shifted to Pier 86 in Seattle to top off with the final 48,000 metric tons of grain. Just as the loading started, we received our official ballots for casting votes on whether the ship should become unionized. I cast my vote and sent it back to the National Labor Relations Board, but we never heard what the final vote tally was, and it didn't matter much anyways as the ship would soon be out to sea.

The final loading was going well until another delay came along —this one happened because of snow drifts blocking the train tracks in Idaho. That meant loading the remaining amount of grain, almost 17,000 metric tons of it, would have to wait. It would take them a few days to clear the train tracks of snow, forcing us to leave and anchor in nearby Elliot Bay.

After we were anchored safely, some U.S. Marshals came up the gangway during my watch and flashed their badges at me on deck, saying they were seizing the ship for unpaid wages. If anyone aboard thought this was going to end easily, they were sadly mistaken. The seizure was being demanded by the last tank cleaning outfit used in Portland, and they wanted $725,000 to pay off the remainder of their cleaning bill. They had obtained a court order placing the ship under federal jurisdiction, with the order allowing the ship's owner to post a bond for the disputed amount. Then the dispute would be settled in civil court at a later date. The U.S. Marshals went up to discuss this with the captain, and placed a warning over the ship's helm about not moving the ship in the meantime.

We also found out from a Seattle newspaper that the first tank cleaning outfit had been given a fine for every illegal worker they'd hired, plus an extra fine for each individual violation, which totaled up to be $242,000. Was anyone going to have any money left over before this was completed?

Our bad luck changed for the better the following week, when the grain arrived from Idaho and a bond had been posted for the cleaning bill. The end to this nightmare was near! The ship was allowed to dock at Pier 86 in Seattle again and we commenced loading the grain. It took only three days to top off the tanks with the final amount, finishing exactly two months over the contracted timeline, but we were fully-loaded and ready to sail. All the legal maneuvering concerning the cargo, the ship's purchase and contract, the tank cleaning with injured workers, plus the results of union voting, would all be settled after we were long gone from Seattle and well out of U.S. waters.

But before departing, we still needed to load the necessary supplies for the trip to Karachi, where the ship was scheduled to be anchored thirty-five miles offshore. From there the grain would be transferred into smaller ships for delivery into the various river ports along the coast. So for the long trip ahead we began bringing aboard the food and supplies, including two full crates of alcohol. All the labels were on the outside of the cartons as they came aboard the ship, so there was no mistaking what we had. They even seemed to add in additional supplies for Pakistan, it was something extra for the four months needed to unload the grain while at anchor. One of the A/B's even decided to buy a Nintendo Entertainment System and asked me to chip in on the cost along with the other A/B's—which we did.

After we departed Seattle and made it out past the Strait of Juan de Fuca, we headed south along the U.S. coastline. I was surprised by this, thinking we'd take more of a great circle course across the Pacific, and then angle down towards Japan, through the South China Sea, and then on to our first stop in Singapore. Instead, we were going well east of Hawaii and out into the doldrums of the Pacific—where few ships, and even fewer ports, were located.

Eventually at sea the captain decided that the A/B's wouldn't stand bridge watches anymore due to the lack of shipping traffic, so us mates stood our watches on the bridge all alone. That meant each of us was the mate, the helmsman, and the lookout—all at the same time—with no one to watch over things when we went to the bathroom (the *head* in nautical terms). I was reminded of this one night while using the head when I heard someone come up on the bridge, walk around, and then pause. A minute later I heard the same footsteps coming my way, walk down the stairs, and disappear down below. They never asked if anyone was around while the ship went full steam ahead with nobody watching. It's a good thing I didn't die while sitting inside the head or else they would have found out about it when the second mate came up to relieve me at midnight.

The ship, even though fully-loaded, still picked up other targets on radar at great distances. I picked up one ship while standing my watch alone at nearly twenty-four nautical miles away from us, then tracked it using the radar's collision avoidance system. It kept showing a CPA (closest point of approach) as being 0.0 between us, which meant we were either going to have a collision or a near miss—so one of us needed to change course.

The second mate was coming up to relieve me for dinner, so I bumped over the auto-pilot a couple of degrees to give us a CPA of two nautical miles, and the second mate became unhappy about that, almost laughing. I pointed out we had no helmsman and the other ship was only twelve miles away now, but if he wanted me to change it back to a collision course, I would. Later, when I started back up to the bridge after dinner, that ship was passing us by on the port side, and it was the first ship I'd seen in nearly a week.

The A/B's had been assigned to work with the bosun during this time, and this was while the ship was pitching due to some heavy swells in the area. These were hitting us from head-on, with the distance between swells being quite far apart, which made the bow rise on one swell and then dip after it passed by. But that made the bow rise even higher when it rebounded—and on the following dip, if the next swell hit the ship at that exact moment—it had a chance of rolling over the bow. A few times a swell had come close, and that was when I should've called the captain to close off the main deck from other crewmembers.

Then a while later I saw the bosun with the A/B's walking up forward to the focsle for equipment, and as I watched from the bridge, they safely made it inside the forward hatch. A moment later one of the swells came over the bow and rolled all the way back down the entire length of the deck. Had the bosun and A/B's been out there, they probably would've been killed by it. I told the captain after seeing this and he wasn't very happy with me, but it was a lesson learned.

Unfortunately we still had a casualty though, and it happened while the A/B's were working inside a segregated ballast tank the following day. I was familiar with where they were working, since I'd been inside that tank a few times when we were docked in Portland. After climbing down inside the tank about ten feet, there was a large steel platform with huge holes cut into it to lighten the weight of the plating. Every ten feet down there was another shelf like that, with a steel ladder that reached down to the next level below it. It was easy to see how if someone wasn't careful, they could easily fall through one of the large openings and hit the next level below. Fortunately the openings didn't line up, or else it could be a fall down the entire depth of the tank to a certain death at the bottom.

During a roll from the swells was when one of the A/B's slipped and fell through an opening, then cracked his head on the steel shelf where he landed. The other A/B's got him out of the tank and into the infirmary, where they asked me to care for him, since I was also the medical officer. The radio officer made contact with a doctor at the nearest shore facility, who directed me to take his vital signs every hour, while the captain was instructed to change course and head towards a military base which had a medical team ready.

Once we got close enough to their base two days later, out to sea came a helicopter to pick up the injured crewmember. He was strapped into a stretcher and placed out on the starboard side of the ship's main deck—just like they instructed us to do. When they arrived, the helicopter lowered a long cable that the bosun attached to the stretcher with its hook, and away went the injured worker up into the air. It took a while, but they got him aboard the helicopter safely, and we all gave a sigh of relief on the ship. The last thing we wanted to see was him falling 200 feet onto a steel deck. That must have been one scary trip up from the look of things.

As we continued on and got closer to the equator, we started to get fewer satellite fixes for navigation. In fact, at one point we went a day and a half without a single fix, and nobody had brought a sextant aboard—not me, not the other two mates, and neither had the captain. So without a sextant or the satellite fixes, we had no way of knowing our position other than through dead reckoning. However, I'd seen that old Loran C unit in the back of the chart room earlier, with the appropriate Loran tables in the bookcases nearby. Acting on a whim during my morning watch, I was able to get a Loran C signal and calculate a line of position. Surprisingly it plotted to within five nautical miles of our dead reckoning position at the closest point, pretty good considering that's all we had available.

After watch I decided to play with the Nintendo Entertainment System that we had all paid for to see if it was worth the cost. It was set up in the large rec room for the crew to use, and came with a game called *Zelda II, The Adventures Of Link*. It was about a little boy who had to save a princess, and while I didn't know much about the game, the more I played it, the dumber I felt doing it. And when one of the A/B's suddenly came into the rec room—I felt really stupid as he watched me for a moment and then left without saying anything. That was the last time I ever used the Nintendo machine, imagining all the jokes they told about it while guzzling down alcohol in the berthing areas below.

At this point the company was getting worried about how long the voyage to Singapore was taking, and wanted us to shorten it, if at all possible. Instead of doing the route planning before the start of the voyage, they now asked the captain to check and see if a shortcut could save us time off the trip. I'd also been calculating the best routes along the way, so when the captain told me the company expected us to save a thousand miles, I mentioned it would only happen if we tunneled through the earth. He agreed, and said that's what he'd fax back and tell them.

As we neared the Philippines, one of the A/B's came up to the bridge to relay how all of the booze aboard the ship was suddenly gone—he told me the deck gang had drank everything. When you consider it was two pallet loads plus personal supplies, that was a lot of drinking in a little over three weeks. By chance I'd brought aboard a large bottle of whiskey for myself, which the A/B had noticed me carrying up the gangway in Seattle. Now he came to beg me for it, even wanting to pay anything to get it. Wow, they were getting desperate. Even the captain was drinking on the ship, he seemed to have some with his coffee and cigarettes he smoked throughout the day. I rarely saw him eat a real meal, preferring to either drink or smoke them. Since he'd sold all the spare booze from the ship's store, I ended up giving my bottle of whiskey to the A/B, without asking for anything in return since he was a friend. I knew they'd drink the whole bottle in one night anyways.

Now we were getting enough shipping traffic so that the captain assigned the A/B's to stand bridge watches again. At this point all we had to do was finish sailing down the South China Sea, and then enter the Singapore Straits before hitting port. While on watch during the day, I altered course for a large Chinese junk that was sailing across us, and afterwards the Chinese junk changed its course so we were back on a collision course—forcing me to alter course again to miss it. Later that day when I told the captain about this, he told me to call him up to the bridge the next time they tried that. He said he'd scare the crap out of them for doing it, and I believed him.

Finally! We're almost there! As we entered the Singapore Straits during my evening watch, there was even more shipping traffic around us than I'd seen since leaving Seattle. The A/B on my watch still hadn't actually steered the ship much up to this point, so the auto-pilot was trusted more with him watching the course. The captain was on the bridge when another supertanker passed us by on the port side, I couldn't believe how close she was. Still on auto-pilot and all I saw was a huge shadow move by, lucky for us nothing happened.

When we anchored safely in Singapore harbor, by morning there were locals climbing aboard the ship and setting up shop in the passageways selling electronics, food, clothing, and even their bodies. During the trip down I'd noticed a sudden pain in my left side, it was in the lower intestines, but it hadn't gone away by now. I feared the worst case scenario, which was we depart Singapore and it gets inflamed off Karachi, where we'd be miles out from the nearest port—and probably much further away from any competent medical facility.

As the chief mate had me help load stores that morning while at anchor, it seemed the Sun was directly over our heads so early in the day, and the cargo deck was heating up to over 120 degrees. It all made me feel dizzy, so after this I was allowed to go see a doctor by the captain, and went ashore via a launch to get some tests done.

Once I hit the dock, the whole Singapore waterfront area looked almost sparkling clean. There wasn't trash to be seen anywhere—no beer bottles or candy wrappers on the ground, and the people sitting around the docks seemed to be well-behaved for a port area. They must be pretty strict against crime here, I thought, to keep it like this in such a busy port. At the hospital, I noticed in the front lobby they had Mercedes Benz and Rolls Royce cars parked in a row like it was opening night at the Oscars. Being my first time in Singapore, it seemed to be a very impressive place.

I walked up to the front desk at the hospital and asked the lady if anyone here spoke English, assuming few of them could. The lady ignored me and spoke back in better English than the ship's crew, then directed me to the doctor's office after I gave her my information. Even the doctor spoke perfect English, so we discussed my medical issue at length. Next he pushed down on my lower left side, and again the pain was in that one peculiar spot. He decided to hold me overnight for testing to see what they'd do the next day. Before leaving, I went into his office and told him how the ship was going to Karachi—and I needed to get off. He smiled and waved me away.

They put me in a room with five other patients on an upper hospital floor, where I sat on the bed feeling pretty good, and every so often a nurse would pass by. One pretty young nurse eventually walked up and showed me some medication—so I looked at her and asked what it was. After looking at her clipboard, she quickly walked away with it, and didn't come back. Good thing I asked, it wasn't very reassuring to have this happen in a foreign country. Then an hour later, another nurse showed up with a supervisor, and I again asked what they were giving me. "It's to clean your system," the head nurse said, and boy, did it.

The following morning they took me into a room and gave me anesthesia, then started to shove a scope down my throat. All I remember was gagging pretty badly as this happened, and then waking up later after it was all over. They'd scoped down to check my stomach, and the doctor said it all seemed normal. But he needed to do some further testing to see what was causing the pain, and recommended I be let go by the ship. The agent had called me long-distance and said they wanted me to stay aboard, particularly the owner. But what to do?

I went back out to the ship and met the captain, and gave him the doctor's recommendation. He reluctantly signed me off, saying he wouldn't do it other than he had to be safe. I collected all of my personal belongings and left on a launch, looking back at the ship one last time. She seemed to be so peaceful while sitting at anchor—like a giant resting amongst the many smaller ships floating around her.

Once back at the hospital, they put me in the same room as I'd had before, and did some further medical testing. I stayed one more night and then got a hotel room nearby that was overlooking the harbor area. This was after the doctor told me he couldn't figure out what was causing the pain, so he let me go, but informed me that the ship had already sailed for Karachi that morning. I felt sad in a way, it had been four months since I'd first come aboard her in Portland, and had escaped through the tank cleaning, the injuries, the lawsuits, the union problems, the marshal seizure, and finally making it out to sea after having finished loading. And then to end up here like this.

Back at my hotel room, I decided on a whim to flip through the phone book sitting next to the telephone. *What interesting things were there in Singapore?* I quickly got to the escort section and they had many ads for local services, but I wasn't sure if I was up to it after that hospital stay. I mulled it over while watching TV for an hour, and then decided what the hell.

I called up one number from an ad, while the woman who answered said they had many different nationalities of female escorts available. They had Chinese, German, American, Japanese, and Thai. I told her which one and gave her my hotel information. When the escort showed up, she was with one of the room service workers of all people—I guess to make sure I wasn't Jack the Ripper. Once I let her inside, we agreed on a price and went on with business, but I was glad it was a one-time binge.

I made the plane flight home the next morning on Singapore Airlines, including a stopover in Japan for a couple of hours. There I was able to go and look in all of the shops they had selling every type of electronic gizmo ever made. From there it was on to a stop in Hawaii, and finally back to the mainland of the United States. I don't know what seemed longer, the plane flight back or the ship ride across, but I got home safely and wouldn't you know it, that pain in my side was gone as well.

7

Transporting Lube Oils

After departing the last grain ship, I made it back home healthy and relaxed for a couple of months. Whenever I left a ship, it took time for my body to adjust to sleeping like a normal person again. Usually at sea the most sleep I ever got in any one stretch was about six hours, so I had to take naps at other times to make up for the lack of rest. Then at home, my body had to get over that and learn to sleep for longer periods.

Eventually I called up the agent at the same company to see if he had any openings coming up. In the meantime, they'd replaced the other guy with this new person, and he told me about these changes while we talked over the phone. He also asked me how everything had gone on the last ship, and I casually mentioned being taken off for some medical reasons. His voice instantly changed after hearing this, and he quickly told me that nothing was available for me to sail on. Then I felt dumb for having mentioned my medical issue—and knew I should've lied and said everything had gone perfectly. He then said to call him back in a few months, and he hung up the phone.

But despite how the agent had acted—I did call him back, and it was only one month later, but got the same treatment from the same agent. Nothing was available for some time, he said, so I hung up and prepared my resume to send out elsewhere.

Remembering back to the last time I'd done this, I only sent out my resume to the companies that were hiring, and this time it was much more impressive sounding than the earlier one.

I had sea time listed as a third mate for two different ships, and also sea time as an A/B along with that. Here's how my resume looked when it was finished:

RESUME

MARK HENRY GLISSMEYER

CREDENTIALS:

U.S. Coast Guard, Third mate, Ocean Steam or Motor Vessels, Any Gross Tons; Radar Observer, Unlimited

U.S. Coast Guard, Master, 100 Gross Tons

F.C.C. General Radiotelephone Operator License

LTJG U.S. Naval Reserve

EDUCATION:

B.S. in Nautical Industrial Technology (May 1985), -California Maritime Academy- Graduated 3rd out of fifty-two deck students.

Studied at Colegio Navarrette, 1978-79, in Guaymas, Mexico, to master the Spanish language.

EXPERIENCE:

THIRD MATE:

- Crude Oil Tanker, 268,000 DWT, Largest U.S. Flag Tanker. Cleaned for grain. 1,120 foot overall length
- TAGOS, U.S. Research Vessel under MSC contract for undersea operations. 224 foot overall length

ABLE SEAMAN:

- TAGOS, U.S. Research Vessel under MSC contract for undersea operations. 224 foot overall length

DECK CADET:

- Crude Oil Tanker, 176,000 DWT, Vessel operates on a run between Valdez, Alaska and Panama.

REFERENCES:

Available on request.

****

I put the part about having references available on request because that's what I saw listed on other resumes, but didn't have any actual references ready, and was never asked for them by any company. It seemed like the agents went on a kiss and a promise when it came to what was listed. I added in the part about being a

Master at 100 Gross Tons because technically I was qualified for that, even though I'd never actually sailed as a master. And it seemed to sound good, at least on paper.

A couple of weeks passed by before an agent getting my latest resume suddenly called me up with a job offer. It was for a tanker that ran lube oils between Houston and the West Coast, and he was the same agent that I'd talked with as a cadet. I must've done well with his company, as they seemed to want me back. He told me the deck officers they were hiring now were no longer scabs, and had formed a union, yet it was a shell union and was only applicable to their single company.

That seemed odd?

Next the agent asked me if I was a "union guy", so I quickly needed to come up with the right answer. The one I gave him back seemed obvious—*I would be if needed.* (This allowed me to hedge myself because in the back of my mind, I was thinking they must've hated unions, or else why did they break away from the last one?)

He then told me how to join their union, which meant there were no picket lines to cross like I'd done as a cadet. The union dues were pretty small, about $100 per year, so I did as he asked and soon was scheduled to go aboard the tanker when she arrived in Long Beach.

Six days later I flew down to the LAX airport in the afternoon and took a taxi to the dock where my ship was tied up, then walked aboard her. She seemed similar to the T2 tankers built during World War II, but had a slightly larger design. That meant having a mid-house and an after-house, with a catwalk connecting the two of them. She was one of three sister ships built in the 1950's, and the last of them to still be sailing—with one sister having been scrapped, and the other being burned up in an accident.

This tanker was on a run that carried lube oils to various ports along two different coasts. After finishing up here in Long Beach, she'd next sail south and through the Panama Canal, then north to the Houston Ship Channel where the lube oils would be unloaded.

Then she'd get a new cargo to carry back to the West Coast. They were almost finished loading to start the Panama Canal run, with me coming aboard to relieve the third mate—who was ready to depart for his vacation.

Once aboard I walked forward and entered the mid-house, where I placed my bags in the passageway. I heard someone talking just around the corner, so I walked around and said I'm the new third mate, and my belongings are in the hallway. The person I talked to ended up being the chief mate, and he smiled and welcomed me aboard. Then he told me the person behind him was the captain, who also smiled and said that once I get my sea bags stowed in my cabin—which he pointed to—I could come up to his office and sign on. I thanked them and went into my cabin, where I stowed everything and collected my paperwork.

Once I got up to the captain's office, I knocked on the latched-open door and said hello, since I saw the captain standing over by his desk. He asked me in, then told me the way I'd come aboard his ship was all wrong. "First off, it isn't a hallway out there, it's a passageway. And you aren't the new third mate until I tell you so. Now let's see your paperwork." Is this the same person I'd just talked to ten minutes earlier? There's an old unwritten rule that one never argues with the captain, so I gave him my paperwork without saying a word, and he looked it over. Then the captain signed me on and confirmed I was the new third mate, and I'd be standing the 8:00 to 12:00 watch. Then he reminded me to never come on his ship like that again, and dismissed me.

From there I went below and went into the cargo office, where the departing third mate was seated. We talked for a bit and he told me about the ship—including how all of the tank valves were manually opened and closed out on deck, when suddenly a senior naval officer came behind us in the passageway and said he was the father of a cadet coming aboard. I thought that seemed strange, why would the father show up to look over a ship for a cadet? We talked with him briefly, at least he talked with the out-going third mate while being unimpressed with me—and then he left us. Next the outgoing third mate told me how the ship was almost loaded for her next voyage, and with that I thanked him and we shook hands.

Later that evening was my first watch as third mate on the ship, so I went out to relieve the chief mate on deck. He handed me a loading diagram with all kinds of figures and said I'd be topping off the number four tanks with lube oil, and it was to all be finished during my watch. He said I should first top off the starboard tank by closing off the port side with about five feet to go, and when the starboard tank hits the final reading, I was to open the port tank fully and close the starboard tank after that. I also needed to call the dockworker with an hour to go so he'd be prepared when I shut down loading on the port side, and then again with fifteen minutes left to go as a reminder. When the port tank gets to a half-inch under the final reading, call the dockworker and shut it down. After all the cargo left in the line to the shore facility gets drained into the tank, that should make up for the needed half-inch of cargo. Then close the manifold, and after that the tank valve. He mentioned since he'd also just started loading the forward number two tanks with a different cargo, all I had to do was keep them loading evenly throughout my watch.

"Have you got all of that?" he asked me.

"Yes, I got it."

He then reminded me to call him if I needed any help, even though I knew he'd be asleep and had to get up very early the next morning for another watch. Meanwhile, I noticed a couple of female cadets coming up the gangway, the chief mate said they were here from the U.S. Merchant Marine Academy and would be staying aboard for a couple of months to get sea time. So I guess that was a father checking up on the ship earlier, probably trying to see if this tanker was a safe place for them to work aboard.

After the chief mate left the deck, everything was mine, being on my first watch along with an A/B loading lube oils, and getting ready to top off two tanks. I followed his instructions just like he said—I closed the port tank near the end, then topped off the starboard side, and finally called the dockworker to let him know we had an hour left to go. I carefully watched how fast the final tank filled up, and called the dockworker with fifteen minutes left. With a half-inch left, I called and told him to shut it down. Once the cargo stopped draining into the port tank, I closed the manifold valve and then the tank valve. The final sounding came up just as the chief mate had predicted, it rose a half-inch to its final reading (I used the manual sounding tube to confirm this). Meanwhile, the other two tanks up forward were loading evenly and needed little adjustment before my watch ended at midnight.

The following morning when I relieved the chief mate for my next watch, he asked me how the topping off had gone the night before. He'd been expecting me to call him to help out, and acted all surprised that I'd finished things without him. "No problem," I said, "since you told me just how to do it."

He then said the last lube oils had just finished loading and we were preparing for sea. So I went back to my cabin and took a Dramamine to make sure I was good for the trip out, and notified the engine room about our planned departure. The captain told me that my normal spot when departing or tying up was always at the stern. Once there I'd relay everything to the A/B's on how to handle the mooring lines, with the captain on the bridge giving me orders via walkie-talkie. Departing would be the easiest, with the longshoremen tossing the lines off the dock and into the water, and us winching them aboard or using hand-over-hand on the shorter lines.

After we departed port and once out of the breakwater, we headed south towards Panama, with me standing my 8:00 to 12:00 watch that evening. Then I had my next watch on the bridge the following morning, ate lunch and saw the chief mate in his office, where I asked him for a piping diagram of the ship. In order to do cargo operations, I needed to memorize all the piping in order to load and discharge cargo on my own during watches in port.

With the piping diagram in hand, I learned how the ship had five segregated cargo lines, and they were each painted a different color to help us keep them memorized. There was a light blue, dark blue, yellow, orange, and purple piping that went from the manifold—where cargo hoses are connected from shore—to the individual tanks. The purple line was for a single segregated cargo tank, while the other four colors went to multiple paired tanks. And all of the valves on the ship were operated manually on deck —there was no control room like on the large crude oil tankers. So I went out by the manifold after lunch to study this and to learn where all of the valves were for each of the separate tanks.

As I was standing amidships on the port side reading the diagram, the captain came walking by along the catwalk on his way to the galley to eat lunch. He looked down and saw me, then stopped and asked me if I was looking over the ship's piping. I told him that yes, I was, so he mentioned how he only gives a third mate like me ten days to learn the piping diagram, or else I'd be fired. Then he turned and casually walked away towards the galley. Was I sensing this captain didn't like me much? I hoped not.

The bridge watches aboard ship consisted of the mate on watch along with two A/B's—one A/B was the helmsman by the wheel, and the other was the lookout on the bridge-wing. They would switch jobs every hour to keep the watch moving along, and also to give the lookout time to warm back up if it was cold outside, so technically that meant three people were looking out ahead as we sailed along the coast. It was more than I'd seen on the other ships I'd sailed on besides the Golden Bear, so I probably took it for granted and didn't keep as good a watch as I should've been doing.

A couple of days passed by, when during one night the captain came into the bridge from outside and was angry with me for having spent too much time in the chart room, then he was angry with me for not having the radar set on the twelve-mile scale. He must've been standing out on the bridge-wing watching me and getting nervous, so after chewing me out, he stuck around for over half an hour—and then finally went down below.

We both knew he was right, as I *was* spending too much time in the chart room. And I would learn that the hard way later, but there are two ways to tell a new mate how not to do something. There's the way he did things, and then there's the way that gets the same message across without behaving like a dictator. I later found out from the chief mate that the captain had come up through the hawse pipe (which means he never went through a maritime academy). Instead, he started working aboard ships as an ordinary seaman, and after enough sea time, he moved up to become an able-bodied seaman. After enough sea time and study, he next sat for his third mate's license, then upgraded to second mate after that, then up to chief mate, and finally he became a captain. Maybe that's why he was being tough on me—I went to a maritime academy and didn't earn my license "the hard way" like he did. He certainly acted like that was the reason. I'd been around barely a week and he'd already let me know a couple of times that I might not be staying aboard much longer.

Forgetting that problem, I actually liked the ship—it was refreshing to be on a small tanker that ran along the coast. The cargo piping wasn't too hard to learn, I'd already memorized it even without his "warning", and only had to ask the chief mate about the purple segregated cargo tank, and how it was discharged, to fully understand everything. The manifold on the ship (where cargo hoses are connected from shore) was simple enough to see and use as a guide, so overall I wasn't worried about working in the next port when loading and discharging on my own.

On the trip south, we went along the Mexican coast and then passed by Costa Rica, until we finally made it to the Panama Canal —where we anchored in the Balboa anchorage to await entry into the Pacific locks. Once they were ready to take us into the canal, we raised anchor while the pilots came aboard, then they took control on the bridge and gave us orders for maneuvering the ship into the locks.

The locks used these large moving winches that they called mules to pull the ship through them, and they had Panamanian workers come aboard to handle all the cables being secured to the ship. These Panamanians were some pretty dangerous-looking individuals to have around us, and as third mate, I was stationed at the stern to observe them. I tried to look as tough as I could, but I doubt it was anything that worried these rough and tumble types.

The first locks we went through raised the ship up to the level of Miraflores lake, which we traversed across and then went again through some more locks, which allowed us to pass through the Gaillard Cut. Next we passed into Gatun Lake, which we also traversed across, until we finally arrived into the Atlantic locks on the other side. These dropped us back down to sea-level again, where the Panamanian workers got off and left us.

Once out on the Atlantic side, the pilots got off the ship so we departed and steered north towards Texas—aiming for the Houston Ship Channel. But wow, what rough seas compared to the Pacific side—I'd better take some Dramamine. The winds were coming from across the ocean without any land mass to slow them down, so swells built up in strength and grew huge, and from their direction that put them right on our beam as we sailed north. That meant the ship would be rolling heavily, much like what I'd seen aboard the TAGOS vessel out of Pearl Harbor.

By chance there was another ship leaving the Panama Canal and heading north at the same time we were. They steered in the same direction, but stuck through it even with the heavy rolling. After taking a beating for an hour, our captain put us on a zigzag course hoping we'd roll less and sail faster through the swells. It seemed to be working, with us staying for twelve hours on a Northeasterly course, and then twelve hours heading Northwesterly. And after all that time our two ships met again—crossing back to within a couple of miles from each other. We had matched them in total distance as a crow flies, but had an easier ride of it due to the zigzag route we took, while they toughed it out rolling instead.

While looking at the chart, it showed in this stretch of the ocean it was relatively shallow, where a ship could even drop an anchor and be well over a hundred miles from the nearest land. It was like a reef extended across here to Cuba, and it must have been a good fishing area, as scattered small boats with long fishing nets stretched out in the area. As we entered the Yucatan Channel and passed through towards the Gulf of Mexico, a strong current pushed us off course, so we had to make a course adjustment and get back on our track-line again.

Once we entered the Gulf of Mexico, the seas became much calmer, and eventually we came close enough to the U.S. mainland where the offshore oil rigs started to appear on radar. There were hundreds of them spread out along the coast, and their positions were clearly marked on the chart. With our known course laid out, we could decipher from the radar which oil rigs were ahead of us, as their spacing had enough variation to pick out locations and safely navigate through them along our track-line.

We continued on and picked up the pilot just outside of Galveston, where he directed us into the Houston Ship Channel. When I mentioned to him that this was my first time in the channel, he brought up how we're going to where the 1947 Texas City disaster happened. He said a ship exploding at the dock back then turned into a chain reaction involving many other vessels, and culminated in hundreds of houses being destroyed, along with over 500 people dying. He said the blast was so great they even found a ship's propeller over a mile away from the explosion site. On hearing this, I wondered what our chances were to do the same, but couldn't see much reason to worry about it. The lube oils we carried were difficult to catch on fire—unlike those ships in 1947 that carried ammonium nitrate used in making explosives.

When we got nearer to the dock, the captain eventually sent me back to my station at the stern. On the way there I took a look over the side of the ship, and noticed the water flowing out of the channel seemed to be quite dark with an unnatural appearance to it. Since this was during the heat of summer, I could feel the mugginess in the surrounding air, and just walking around the deck added about fifteen degrees to the already hot day.

The A/B's arrived at the stern with me just in time to tie up the tugboat, then we waited for a while as the pilot maneuvered to get the ship alongside the dock. There was always the fun part of throwing the monkey's fist over to the longshoremen, but these guys were too good at it and rarely came up short. At the maritime academy, the cadets had usually thrown them early and missed into the water, almost like a Hail Mary pass in football. Here the A/B's only did what took the least effort to get the job done—a sign of experience.

Once we tied up the ship, the bosun got the gangway out onto the dock, and within ten seconds the first crewmembers were already ashore. It was the galley crew and a couple of engineers to go first, followed by the radio operator. At every dock this seemed to happen, it was like they all had a hot date at the end of the pier waiting for them in every port.

One of the mates would have to get ready for cargo operations, depending on the time we tied up. I was lucky in that the second mate was on watch now and would be doing this. At first the dock-workers came aboard to discuss things with the captain and chief mate, such as which hoses needed to be connected to the manifold for discharge. If there were any jumper hoses needed, the bosun had already connected those earlier on the way in. Lastly, the engineer on watch would have to be notified which cargo pumps were needed—to get them ready for discharging.

I didn't have to worry about any of this though, since I wasn't coming on watch for another five hours. I went and relaxed for a couple of hours before going to have dinner in the galley. There were fewer crewmembers in port that ate aboard the ship—even the steward would be gone for most meals—but sometimes he switched off with the cook on who had to stay behind and serve.

When it came time to stand my watch, I figured that discharging the cargo was the easier operation compared to loading. There was less chance of an oil spill since the tanks were emptying, and the cargo pumps were doing the hard work. All I had to do was watch things and make sure they stripped out evenly. And that's exactly how my watch would go that night, and the next morning it went the same way as well. I had no problems doing what they expected of me when it came to standing cargo watches, and I didn't hear the captain again about having to learn the cargo piping. Then a new captain came aboard to relieve him, so off he went on his vacation during a scorching afternoon.

On my evening cargo watch, I heard from a couple of returning crewmembers that the others were down below by the dock having some drinks, and they wanted me to head down there after I was finished at midnight. Why not, I thought, so after my watch ended—I headed down to have a beer with them, when our two cadets sailing with us came up in a hurry just after I'd cracked open a beer. Without even getting a sip down, I was already being chewed out by one of them. Apparently the cadets were under the impression that getting a job in the industry was easy, at least they said this after talking with the two captains. Another ship was tied up nearby, so their captain and our captain told the cadets that once a cadet graduates, they're all set in the industry. I knew they were wrong and so were the cadets, but I wisely didn't argue with them. Besides, the cadets appeared to have drunk a lot of beer, too much to reason with, that's for sure.

Eventually we finished discharging cargo and left for another dock deeper in the Houston area by Deer Park. The channel seemed to get more narrow the farther we went inland, with the pilot practically aiming at other ships passing us and then turning away at the last minute. The water in the channel stayed darkish along the way too—I was told that this was actually the cleaned up version compared to fifteen years earlier, when there was raw oil covering the soupy mix we were seeing. After tying up, we finished discharging the last of our cargo, and moved on to the loading dock.

The chief mate had printed up a loading diagram that showed a schematic of the ship along with all of the tanks, and it included the cargo names with quantities to load. It also showed the final tank readings we needed when topping off. Since this was loading, we wouldn't be using any cargo pumps, it would all be entering the ship through the manifold and be distributed to the tanks via the piping system. The key was to keep the cargo in the tanks and not let it overflow when topping off, and to get each tank to the correct reading that the chief mate had calculated for us.

Since I'd already done some topping off when I first came aboard, I wasn't worried about handling my end of things. The procedure was the same as in Long Beach—just have the chief mate tell me what was needed when I relieved him for watch, and follow his directions. We loaded half the cargo at one dock, then shifted closer towards Galveston for the remainder of the lube oils.

One thing I noticed while on watch at night was the mugginess sticking around in the air, and how certain pests arrived every night just before I got off watch. While out on deck, I could see them spreading around as swarms, slowly coming over the ship like a fog bank and descending upon the whole area. It seemed like these millions of mosquitoes would arrive out of nowhere, to start landing on any exposed skin we had. I never found out if these were saltwater or freshwater mosquitoes, but they behaved like hungry ones either way. I was lucky to be getting relieved by the second mate just as they became unbearable, and happily they were gone by the next morning.

After two days at the dock, we finished loading early in the morning and prepared to head out for sea. But once the pilot came aboard, he said we'd have to wait it out in Galveston while Hurricane Chantal passes over the area. We could already see the heavy rain and increasing winds arriving, and the channel was more choppy as we navigated out.

After we tied up in Galveston, the winds were still getting stronger outside. The dock was situated so that the strengthening gusts held us firmly against the dock, but it ended up being a false sense of security. Later, when I took over the morning watch, it was raining very hard and the winds were now almost hurricane strength, with gusts peaking over sixty-five knots. I was observing all of this from under the ship's overhang, when the eye of the hurricane suddenly came over us. The strong winds died down to blue skies, and it became very calm and peaceful outside. I stepped out onto the main deck to admire the sunshine coming from within the eye of the storm above. It was how they'd described things to us at the academy—you get a lull with sunshine and then the winds hit again.

And that's exactly what happened. Suddenly the winds came back just as strong, but this time they were coming from the opposite direction. Oh hell! The ship started to blow off the dock now, and the mooring lines began to stretch and strain like they'd break at any moment. I ran up to the captain's office and told him we had to double-up the lines, then ran back and got the A/B on watch to help me. The three of us together got out the extra

120

mooring lines just in time, with the A/B having his hat blow off in the process. At seventy knot winds, it must have gone far, but at least the ship didn't break away from the dock and follow behind it.

After the hurricane finally passed, the pilot came aboard and took us out past the breakwater. We'd escaped any hurricane damage, but the pilot said many homes in the area were ruined due to the rainfall, and some people had died as a result. Maybe that's why I noticed there weren't any trees over fifteen feet tall growing in the surrounding areas. If they had hurricanes passing over like this one, I could see why.

Once we dropped off the pilot, we continued out and headed south towards the Panama Canal. Along the way and after we'd passed through the Yucatan Channel, we got back into the same area where I'd seen those small fishing boats earlier on the trip up north, with their long fishing nets being supported on the water by small red floats. I'd avoided them the last time through, but the ocean now seemed choppier, and it made seeing the little floats even harder.

Eventually there was a fishing boat up ahead during my watch —but I couldn't see any nets. The boat was off the starboard bow, and as we got closer, suddenly the red floats appeared crossing our path. I could see someone on the fishing boat watching our ship, so I had the helmsman go into hand steering and put the rudder over left to twenty degrees, and kept it there until the ship was turning enough so we'd be on a path to just miss the end of the nets. Next I had him ease the rudder to ten degrees, and finally went amidships just as we steered by them.

Once past the nets, we swung back to our normal course and I had the helmsman put her back on the auto pilot. Whew, I thought, we'd just missed dragging those nets for a couple of miles back there. At least I saved that fisherman a lot on money in repairs. We continued on and luckily that was the last encounter I had with those small fishing boats. They always seemed to be working that one area over a shallow reef, perhaps there was a nearby village somewhere?

I stood my next watch that night with no more troubles, and came back the next morning for my usual time. After I was up on the bridge for an hour, the new captain showed up and pointed me back into the chart room. After closing the drapes behind us, he asked me if I'd done a quick course change the day before, so I explained turning the ship to avoid those fishing nets. Suddenly he got angry and said I'd almost lost the ship's plant by doing that, and I was never to turn the ship like that again. He said if I see any fishing nets out ahead of us again, just run them over. Then he left in a huff, and went down below. All I could think was—oh no, not this one too!

By chance I had another unfortunate experience come up the next day while on watch, something that the older A/B at the helm was nice enough to warn me about. He said the younger A/B was relaying everything I said back in the crew's mess. I'd often talked with the younger A/B during watch when he was at the helm and there was nothing out there. Usually we had conversations about the industry and ports we'd visited, or about women and world events. But apparently everything was coming out the way he wanted things to be, not necessarily what I was saying. So it was spreading amongst the crew, even if it was something meant to be personal.

After learning of this, I limited talking to the younger A/B during our watches for that very reason, and he got mad at me for avoiding him. No matter what, it seemed, I couldn't win here. But it was a lesson learned—and it showed how everything said on a ship gets spread around like the plague, but it wouldn't happen to me again.

We stayed on course and a couple of days later entered the anchorage at Colon, where we waited for the pilots and authorization to enter the Panama Canal. Eventually the pilots came aboard after we weighed anchor, and they took us into the locks as we started across the isthmus of Panama. This was the hottest time of year to be crossing, with the Sun directly overhead and no clouds to be seen anywhere. I was surprised during the last trip through that I hadn't seen any mosquitoes, but this time was different.

There were many of them swarming around, and it was happening in broad daylight.

Eventually I was bitten by one of the passing swarms, and it was a very large mosquito that got me. Back at the maritime academy we'd read about what it took to build the Panama Canal, and how lots of men had died during its construction. One of the issues they faced were the diseases those men got from being bitten by mosquitoes, so I was obviously worried about my health after this.

One of the two cadets had come back to the stern with me while we passed through the locks, and when we went into the galley, I noticed she had a frightened look on her face. She said some of the Panamanian workers were staring at her through the portholes. When I turned around, I could see their faces; they looked like they'd never seen a woman before, much less a young one that was this pretty—and they were scary-looking as hell. I quickly walked over and closed the drapes over them, then took her up forward to the bridge, just to make sure the Panamanians didn't try anything. After we made it through the Panama Canal, we dropped off the pilots and then headed north, on a track-line for our next port in Southern California.

During my time off at sea, I had to do the basic chores like a person does when living at home. Each cabin for the officers had its own head, and for laundry we had a communal washing machine and dryer in the passageway by the second mate's cabin. I saved up my dirty laundry and tried to do a normal-sized load whenever I used them, but for some reason lately there seemed to be a large load running whenever I wanted to use the laundry. The front of the machines had clear glass so everyone could see whatever was inside, meaning a crewmember couldn't keep any secrets with what was tumbling in there. One of the women aboard was doing lots of laundry it seemed, so I went into the rec room where the two cadets were watching TV, and asked them if they were responsible for all of the large loads of panties I kept seeing. They just laughed and shook their heads no.

The rec room was near the small office where we kept the logbook while doing cargo operations, and was also across from a stairway. Whenever someone came down from the bridge or the captain's office—they arrived in the passageway at the rec room, so whoever was sitting inside there would be seen. They had a large TV in the rec room with shelves full of VHS movies on the back bulkhead, and various crewmembers had brought many of them aboard, including some porno tapes—with about ten of those available to watch.

I had already seen a few of the porno tapes while aboard out of curiosity, and there was one porn star who was particularly pretty in one of them. One day while on my bridge watch, I mentioned this to the captain, and how she'd performed something special in the tape. Well, the next day while passing by the rec room, I checked—and that porno tape with her in it was missing. I knew the captain had his own TV with a VHS player in his cabin, so he must have taken the tape? And not only that, but it never appeared back in the rec room for the duration of the trip while I was aboard.

On the way north, we passed by some small fishing boats similar to the ones I'd barely avoided on the trip south, but I didn't get close enough to have to worry about their fishing nets. There was a large sailboat that called our ship on the radio though, asking if we'd seen any winds in the past couple of days. There was an unusual calm on the ocean that made it look like a glassy mirror, and the sunlight would reflect off that and almost blind our eyes. I told him how I hoped he had lots of booze and women aboard, because we hadn't seen any winds since we'd left Panama.

The rest of the trip towards Long Beach was uneventful, and by then the welt that I'd received from that mosquito bite was finally going down. Not only was that a huge mosquito that had bitten me, but the welt I received was equally enormous and long-lasting. I didn't get any chills or fever from it, although once I woke up very pale for some strange reason, and hadn't looked that bad in a long time, almost like I was death warmed over. After eating breakfast, I felt much better, and it didn't happen again for the remainder of the trip.

We were scheduled to get a new chief mate and pumpman in the next port, so when we arrived in Long Beach and docked, the departing chief mate came up and told me I'd done an amazing job as third mate. *Really?* He hadn't said anything about my job performance up to then, and neither had any of the other crewmembers outside of the captain. I actually thought they felt the opposite way, but I replied "Thank you, I tried my best," just before he left the ship.

The new chief mate was already down with the second mate on deck, and when I walked up to him, he recognized me. We had sailed together on the oil tanker that ran up to Valdez when I was a cadet. What a small world! He said how he remembered me, and I joked about the grades he'd given me while on that tanker. Lucky for me he laughed back. Later I found out the chief mate had been promoted to captain on a different tanker after that, but the ship had blown up while entering a port. He had been demoted back down to chief mate as a result, at least that's how I heard it. From my experiences so far, I could see how easy it was to have an accident aboard a ship. It almost seemed inevitable for anyone sailing long enough at sea, especially for a tanker mate.

We stayed and discharged in Long Beach, using different docks depending on what they needed for cargo. The two cadets had gone ashore to visit the San Diego Zoo, and after they'd returned, one of them told me that on the trip back they were dropped off a long distance from the dock. While walking back to the ship along the back streets, a car had started to follow them, so they ran for their lives to get away and had just made it back aboard safely.

After Long Beach, we went up the California Coast to Martinez, which meant a trip under the Golden Gate Bridge. I had already been under the bridge a few times while aboard our training ship, so was familiar with this area. We picked up the pilot at the San Francisco Sea Buoy after calling into the Vessel Traffic Service, then proceeded to go under the bridge and pass Alcatraz Island on our port side. Every time I'd been by here it was windy, with many sailboats out on the water, and other ships moving in and out. If a sailboat was looking to cross ahead of a ship, they often blasted their ship's whistle to warn them about it.

We turned later and went up the North Bay towards the Carquinez Bridge, right by where I'd attended the California Maritime

Academy. As we passed by the campus, I saw the Golden Bear tied up in Morrow Cove, and there were some cadets seen walking among the many pathways and buildings. It brought back fond memories to me, both good and bad, but what a feeling to be sailing by while on a commercial tanker. We continued on up the strait, then tied up at Martinez.

This refinery we docked at had heavy security, and it was a long walk to get out of the complex. I'd asked the two cadets if they wanted to have some pizza with me, and once the gangway was out, I was free to go ashore and go shopping with them. We stopped and picked up some things at the grocery store in town, including a bottle of champagne, then went over to a pizza place just a couple of blocks up the hill. Once inside, we ordered some pizza, but the place was totally empty of other customers.

An older couple was running it apparently, and the man decided to go over to an old organ and entertain us with some music. It was playing so loud that we could barely hear ourselves talk, when one of the cadets lit a cigarette. Then out of the clear blue my parents showed up through the front door looking for me. I was very surprised, as I had no idea they were coming up to see me, much less find me somehow in this pizza place away from the dock. I introduced them to the two cadets, and then I left with my parents—to take them to the ship and show them what my working life was like. We made it through the refinery security and went aboard, and we visited my living quarters, the rec room, the laundry, and we went up to the bridge. I could tell from where the chief mate was standing up forward what cargo operations he was up to, so pointed that out to my parents.

We then went back to the galley to see where I ate my meals, and also went back aft to look out over the stern. I knew I had to relieve the chief mate soon, and that meant we had no time to go back into town and have a better dinner, so my parents left after we said good-bye, and I ate something from the refrigerator on the ship. We stayed in Martinez for two days of cargo operations, then departed and headed back out to sea.

After we passed under the Golden Gate Bridge, I was on watch when the pilot left the ship and the captain went down below. On the chart, it showed shipping lanes to follow depending on which direction we wanted to sail once outside—we could either leave in the southern lane, the northern lane, or the western lane. Since we were going back to Long Beach, we were taking the southern lane. I told the A/B at the helm what course to steer, and went back into the chart room to double-check things. A minute later I heard the U.S. Coast Guard calling our ship on channel 16, and it sounded urgent. I picked up the radio handset and replied back to the Coast Guard, saying I was the third mate. They asked me if I was on the right course, saying they showed the ship heading back towards the Golden Gate Bridge on their radar. When I looked out the front windows of the bridge, I saw we were doing a large circle —and the A/B at the helm had the ship turning back towards Alcatraz Island!

I thought of what to say and quickly told the Coast Guard that everything was fine, we were just testing out the steering gear and would be back on our course shortly, and thanked them. Then I walked over to the A/B and told him to give me fifteen degrees of right rudder. Slowly the ship stopped turning to port and we started to swerve back to starboard. I watched the ship's heading, and as we got closer to the right course, I had him ease the rudder to ten degrees, and then told him the heading we needed.

For someone who hasn't steered a ship before, it's easy to get confused and try to turn the ship around the compass—as though the compass card moves with rudder commands—instead of the ship. That's exactly what the A/B had done, trying to turn the compass card while steering. But it never works, and actually makes things worse, since the helmsman panics. Luckily, there were no other ships around when that happened to him, but it's something I filed away for the next time—remember to wait until the A/B is actually on our course before stepping away.

Once we made it back to Long Beach, we prepared to load cargo for the trip to Houston. I noticed from the loading diagram that we were to get a familiar cargo. Earlier in Houston, we'd loaded almost one-third of the ship with this exact same lube oil, then proceeded to carry it through the Panama Canal, and dis- charge it here in Long Beach. Now we were loading the exact same cargo at a dock less than a quarter of a mile away, to carry it through the Panama Canal—to be discharged back in Houston? Did the oil companies know this even happens?

I pointed this out to the chief mate when I saw him, and he told me that I was being paid to do it, so don't ask questions. So we loaded the ship with that cargo and the other lube oils, then headed out south towards Panama. After a couple of days out at sea, I asked one of the two cadets if she wanted to drink some champagne with me after I got off watch at midnight. She declined—so I let it go, and thought little of it after that. She apparently hadn't forgotten, because the next day she wanted to drink champagne with me and the other cadet. Unfortunately, I knew that three's a crowd and I couldn't risk doing it without getting fired by this captain, so it was my turn to decline.

Later when we were passing by Acapulco, I called the captain up to the bridge at night after getting up on watch, as there was a strange ship doing some crazy maneuvers that I couldn't figure out. He came up quickly and I pointed him to where the ship was, then he went out on the port wing for about five minutes. Afterwards he came back in and said it's nothing to worry about, then went back down below. He didn't seem too concerned about the ship and he turned out to be right—we passed by the ship and continued on.

The next day while on my morning watch, the captain came up to the bridge and took me into the chart room, where he told me to never call him again between eight and nine o'clock at night— no matter what. That was his time and he never wanted to be disturbed again during that hour, then he left the bridge. I thought how strange that was, and wondered what was so important happening between eight and nine o'clock at night?

Sometimes in rough seas we could be on a course where the ship rode very smoothly, almost like someone was floating in a warm bathtub while enjoying it. But then we'd change course and the seas would start the ship rolling, sometimes severely. Since the ship's track-line was already laid out on the chart, I could tell when I had to change course up ahead to maintain the next leg of the voyage. And while heading south there was a course change coming up just before I was getting off my watch at noon—which placed it just prior to lunchtime. I could tell by the swells that we'd be rolling heavily on the new course, but it's the direction we needed to go, and I had no power to change that.

So when I changed course just before lunch, the ship immediately started rolling heavily—after being practically rock-steady prior to that. Once the second mate relieved me on the bridge, I went back to the galley to eat lunch. When I arrived in the officer's mess, the steward was upset with me—a huge pot of chicken noodle soup on the stove hadn't been secured, and after my course change, it had gone right off the stovetop with the first roll. The cook was busy mopping up gallons of soup from the deck and not looking happy at me, so I apologized and said the next time I'd call back to warn them. But it really wasn't my fault we had no soup for lunch, and did they really think I did that course change on purpose?

The new pumpman they'd brought aboard had come through a different union than the regular A/B's working on the ship, and apparently their two unions hated each other. Each time I saw the pumpman on deck lately, he'd made some crack about the A/B's on the ship, and some of them were racist in nature. How he'd made it this far without being punched yet, showed how well restrained the deck crew was. That's when I went to the chief mate and told him how the pumpman was being racist towards the African-Americans on the crew. I said it might be wise to replace him if they didn't want things to escalate, and he told me he'd look into it.

Finally we arrived outside the Panama Canal during the early evening, so we anchored in Balboa harbor to await the pilot. In the meantime, there were over a dozen other ships already in the anchorage—waiting like we were—all spaced apart peacefully and illuminated with deck lights. Then during my anchor watch up on the bridge the next morning, I heard one of the other ships calling on the radio and asking if anyone knew where all the garbage was coming from within the anchorage.

When I looked back towards the stern, I saw plastic bags filled with garbage floating away from our ship. The new steward's assistant had tossed our garbage over the side while in the harbor as though we were still out at sea, and it was being blown towards the other ships downwind from us. I didn't respond to the call on the radio, but only listened, and fortunately they couldn't figure it out, as the floating garbage quickly blew far enough away that it wasn't obvious who'd done it.

In the afternoon the pilots came aboard and we entered the Panama Canal, then passed through and departed safely on the Colon side. Again we encountered extremely rough seas upon leaving in the open ocean, and at night the captain came up to the bridge during my watch, and asked for the key to the medical locker. Being the third mate, I was in charge of the medical supplies aboard the ship, and I had to inventory them and keep track of expiration dates. There was a log of who used what supplies, and how much time was left before reordering. The captain took my key and went for some Dramamine, then gave me the key back later. Even the other mates were feeling the effects of the swells this time, and both looked green at the gills when I saw them during watch changes. Since I'd already taken a dose of Dramamine before departing, the ocean swells weren't bothering me, having already learned my lesson the hard way.

Unfortunately a couple of days later, I bit down on something hard during supper and broke off a part of my bottom molar, so I told the captain about it. It was obvious I needed to see a dentist when we hit our next port in Houston, since without a fix I'd end up in massive pain. He said it would be arranged and I held on, getting lucky in not having much swelling or pain so far.

The closer we got to Houston on this leg, the higher the clouds seemed to rise into the sky amongst the hot air outside. These were the solitary clouds with dark linings that had rain showers coming out, with gusty winds surrounding them. While walking back on the main deck in the afternoon, one of these clouds was passing over the ship, and I heard a thundering boom hit us. Then I smelled the ozone in the air, and knew it was due to lightening hitting the main mast of the ship. One of the engineers came up out of the engine room and asked me if I'd heard an explosion, and I told him it was a lightening strike. For him to hear it while inside that noisy engine room with earplugs on, showed how loud it was. And just the thought of being so close to the mast when the lightning hit was scary enough for me.

After we tied up in Texas City, a taxi came out to take me to the dentist. The captain told me the company would pay for any dental work I needed, and they'd already picked out a dentist for me in a location by Houston. Once I got in the taxi and we started out, the taxi driver brought up how he was a major league baseball fan, and asked me what I thought of the Houston Astros. I told him which state I was from and how I only followed the teams during my vacations, but wouldn't be a fan of the Astros. Yet he insisted to know more, so I told him the rest. Then he got defensive and warned me not to go into any bars, and even called the team I like cheaters after that.

When we finally reached the dentist's office, it was out in a poor area by the outskirts of the city. I couldn't believe it. There was a graveyard, and the office itself was propped up on cinder blocks. This wasn't a good start to the visit, they must have picked the cheapest dentist they could find. Once inside I learned it was a father and son operation, and I was to have my tooth fixed by the son. He took an x-ray of the broken back molar and told me it needed a pin screwed in with a temporary cap over it, and that should last until I got back home.

I told him that sounded reasonable, so he proceeded with the pain shots. Even though he tried his best to scare me about my chances of success, he did a good job placing the pin and capping it off, so I was all set to go back to the ship. The same taxi driver was waiting there and took me back, but we didn't talk about baseball again, which was a good thing for me.

After getting back to the ship, I told the captain about the dentist doing a good job and how I was all set to stand my watch that evening. He informed me that the pumpman was being let go and we'd get a replacement for him sometime the following day. I stood my evening watch with no ill effects from the dentist, just as the two cadets left the ship and were headed for another ship to continue with their sea time. We stayed another day until we shifted docks during the late afternoon. Since tying up had taken longer and continued past dinner, the captain instructed the galley to hold food over and feed us once we got finished. The engineers had already eaten at their normal time, so it was just me and the chief mate sitting at separate tables in the officer's mess once we arrived.

The captain's table was situated at the far end of the officer's mess, with his seat by the back bulkhead so the captain could watch over us while he was eating. The chief mate was always seated across from his spot at the same table. I sat at the middle table and could only see the back of the chief mate when he was present. The third table was for the engineers—except for the chief engineer—who always sat by the captain.

The steward kept the dinner menu near the entry to the kitchen with a few different choices available, and most of us always ordered the same items once we learned what tasted good. On this night I requested roast beef with mashed potatoes and green beans. The cook took my order and put gravy over the roast beef and mashed potatoes on my plate, then added the green beans, and placed it in front of me. I thanked him and carried it over to my table—where I sat down to start eating.

For a moment I paused and got a fork, then decided what to eat first. I looked over the food and thought something seemed different—then I noticed it. Staring back at me on top of the roast beef was a large cockroach, almost as if it was placed there as an hors d'oeuvre. It was as large as any I'd ever seen, and almost looked at peace with itself, but with its legs extended like it was ready to jump at me. It had obviously been sautéed in the gravy they made, which was a thin, watery sauce just poured over the meat. Yet the dead cockroach almost looked happy, probably feeling no pain in its last moments of life. Since I couldn't believe what I was seeing on my plate, I thought of what to do. After a few moments of thinking about it, I got up and walked over to the chief mate seated all alone at the other table.

You couldn't miss noticing the chief mate anywhere since he was a very large man, I'm guessing he carried over 100 pounds of extra weight, and always chewed on dinner like he was severely underweight and starving. I could see he was busy munching his roast beef, so I got up behind him and bumped him on his left shoulder with my plate of food. He looked back with a dirty look like I'd better not bother him anymore or he'd bite my head off. Then I waited a couple of seconds and bumped his shoulder in the exact same spot again. This time he looked back even angrier, but also glanced down at my plate of food. He was still chewing when he noticed the huge cockroach looking back at him. In mid-chew he stopped eating, and that angry face turned into a sickened one —he seemed almost in shock.

I didn't say anything as he knew all I needed to tell him, and I went back over to my chair and sat down. He quickly got up and left the mess without saying a word to me. I thought he might be going to throw up somewhere, since he'd just swallowed some of the same gravy that the cockroach had died in. But I was still starving, and this was all the food I had. I went over to the trash can and took my fork, then slid the road beef with the cockroach on top all into the trash. Now I could sit down and start to eat the rest of my dinner.

A couple of minutes went by until I saw the side door open with the captain leading the chief mate into the officer's mess. The captain gave me a sickened look and asked, "Where is it?"

I told him I needed to eat my dinner so I'd thrown the cockroach into the garbage. There was no need to save it since the chief mate had already seen it. The captain then went into the kitchen and talked with the cook. I didn't follow him or even get up, as I wanted to stay out of this and finish what little dinner remained. I was only a third mate after all, and how it happened was none of my business.

Yet this wasn't the first time I'd been offered questionable food aboard a ship, and it seemed like the captains never did anything about it. They could be tough as nails when disciplining someone like me, but acted like a mouse when it came time to monitor the galley staff. I suspected they were afraid of getting something placed into their food for their troubles, and that was probably a legitimate fear to have. That's why I stayed out of it, I'd rather have the captain take the heat for a change and not me, especially about something like this.

After we finished discharging all the lube oils in port, I got a loading diagram and we prepared the ship for our next cargo. The chief mate was responsible for this by calculating where to load the lube oils and in what volumes, then printed that up for us to go by. Right before we started loading according to his diagram, the chief mate came into the rec room where the second mate was with me, and got mad at us for not noticing how he'd done the calculations wrong. It showed one row of tanks being barely loaded, while the surrounding tanks were nearly filled to the top, which placed too much stress on the bulkheads separating the tanks. He said to check all the cargo diagrams we get in the future, and let him know if anything ever looks wrong again—then he calculated a new one and we were all set to go. We completed loading using two different docks and were shut down only once for lightning in the area, which was good.

We left port fully-loaded and steered south towards the Panama Canal. After a couple of days out at sea, the chief mate came up to me and said the two cadets who'd left us were already on their next ship, but they were saying bad things about us, and their captain was relaying all of this back to our captain. It was amazing how everything went around on these ships like that, proving it's never wise to say something bad about a ship you've just left, thinking they'll never find out about it.

As we passed through the Gulf of Mexico, the weather was much calmer than usual for the area, with a glassy surface on top of the ocean everywhere. Then I smelled a strong odor of petroleum fumes when walking out on the catwalk, and saw a heavy sheen on the ocean nearby—perhaps an oil tanker passing through earlier was cleaning tanks? After a while the sheen became even darker and thicker, and it was spread out about 200 yards across and miles long as we got farther away from the coast. Whoever did it was on the same or opposite course we were, as the sheen stayed alongside us for some time. If someone had thrown a lit match on top of that oil slick, it would've burned to both horizons, and maybe even farther. That was a lot of oil on the ocean needing to dissipate, and must have lingered in the area for days after we'd left. (With the poor sea life getting coated by it and probably dying as a result).

We eventually passed through choppy waters in the Yucatan Channel and made our way into the Colon anchorage area to drop anchor during my morning watch. The captain came up to the bridge to give orders, and told me to go up on the flying bridge and raise the quarantine flag. It was very windy up there, as not only was the ocean showing large whitecaps, but things blew stronger above as the wind got higher up on the ship.

I got the quarantine flag out of the locker and went out above the bridge, then attached it to the only lanyard that was available. As I started to raise the flag up, it occurred to me that I should stop since the course of the ship was blowing the flag towards the radar tower. If only I'd listened to myself, as once I resumed raising the flag—my worst nightmare materialized, and it got too close to the radar tower—and instantly began wrapping itself around the spinning antenna.

In a flash I jumped down and entered the bridge, then quickly shut off both radar units completely. That surprised the captain standing there, and he quickly asked me why I'd just done that. I explained how the wind took the flag into the antenna on the radar tower, and unless they were shut off, it might damage the units. For this one he didn't bother to chew me out, instead he only shrugged about it while continuing to go into the designated area before dropping anchor. Later, after my watch ended, one of the A/B's came up and unwound the flag from the antenna, and then they restarted the radars. So at least my quick thinking saved any damage to them, but the captain got a good chuckle out of it at my expense.

Once we made it through the Panama Canal, we started sailing north towards California again. I was finally going to be relieved when we hit the next port, and was looking forward to this stretch being over with, so I could fly home for my much needed vacation. After two days at sea, we went into an area where the small fishing boats congregated with their long nets, and as I tried to see them up ahead in the choppy waters, one eventually showed up just off the starboard bow.

As we got closer to the fishing boat, I couldn't see where his nets were since the small ocean waves crested higher than the red floats holding up the netting. When the floats finally appeared dead ahead, that's when I noticed they stretched all the way across us from port to starboard. It was too late to try a fast turn to avoid hitting them, so instead I walked out onto the starboard bridge-wing and just watched them get closer.

After another minute our bow finally hit into the long line of nets, and the little red floats holding them up started to wiggle and be pulled towards us. Then our ship began pushing the nets ahead for a distance, until I finally saw them break apart. We left all of the little buoys still floating on the fishing boat side, but on the other side, many of them had disappeared underwater, and the netting that remained was stretched out and partially sunk. The fishing boat itself seemed perfectly fine, except for having its nets cut right down the middle like that.

I went back inside the bridge and shrugged at the A/B, acting like there wasn't any time to miss that one. Suddenly, over the marine radio came someone screaming our ship's name, followed by some cursing and warnings how we'd better turn around. I turned down the volume and listened for a minute—it was obviously from the person aboard the small fishing boat with his nets cut in half—he was trying to get me to somehow turn back while speaking in both Spanish and broken English. After a couple of minutes with no reply, he started to threaten me how he'd find out where we're headed and have me arrested there.

I turned off the volume on the radio and went back to watching ahead for any other fishing boats and shipping traffic. After ten minutes I turned the radio volume back up and the guy was still yelling our ship's name, so I turned it back down again. Ten minutes later when I checked again—he'd stopped—so I placed the volume back to normal, and that was the last I ever heard of him.

We eventually made it safely to the Port of Long Beach, where I was relieved by a new third mate recently hired by the company. I told him about the ship and how to handle cargo operations, just like the earlier third mate had done for me, and then I was paid off by the captain. On the plane flight home, I wondered if things could get any more exciting and stressful than on the trip I'd just finished—I didn't think they could—but sure enough, I was wrong —and would soon find out on my next trip out to sea.

8

With MTBE Aboard

After I was relieved as third mate on the last ship, I needed some vacation time to recuperate from all of the excitement and wonderment I'd experienced. Well, that was the plan anyways, until the agent phoned me seven days after arriving at home. He wanted me to fly to Los Angeles and board a different ship for a week—just to sit at anchor. I explained how I'd barely left the last ship and was hoping to relax, I wasn't even able to get more than six hours of sleep at a stretch while my body adjusted off its watch routine. He again said he needed me—but if I didn't go—he'd have to hire another third mate to do it. That's just what I needed, another split-second decision that might decide my entire future. Still being so tired from the last trip, I told him to go ahead and hire someone else. Yet after I hung up the phone, doubts quickly crept into me that I'd made the wrong decision yet again. And yes, as I later found out, he eventually held it against me.

Luckily the agent did pencil me in for another trip though, and nearly three months later, I got another call from him telling me to fly down to Los Angeles and board the same coastal tanker that I'd sailed on earlier. They wanted me there right after the ship docked to work cargo operations. Was the guy who relieved me not doing so well?

When I got to the ship, I quickly learned that the captain was the same one who'd scolded me for not knowing how to come aboard the last time. He really wasn't my favorite, but maybe things would be better this time around—at least I hoped so. It was also the same chief mate aboard as well, and he explained how they'd just finished coming through the Panama Canal, so the ship was fully loaded. This was a familiar dock to me since the ship always seemed to hit the same spots on each run. Usually we worked each of them a couple of days, but sometimes less, depending on the cargo operations.

After relieving the third mate for his vacation, I started working my regular schedule just like the last time when I was aboard. I stood a watch that evening and then the next morning, until I happened to be tasked with stripping the last two tanks before we sailed for our next port. The first two hours of my watch were spent bringing down the tank levels, then stripping the starboard tank dry. Next I called the dockworker and told him we were approximately an hour away from finishing the last tank. He casually mentioned that they might be having some trouble back up at the plant—something about a possible spill—but he didn't say if it had anything to do with us. With fifteen minutes left, I called the dockworker again to check and he said there was definitely something happening up there, and they might be shutting us down at any moment. I knew that the last tank had less than a foot of cargo left to strip, and to stop now meant either we'd leave with a partial load, or be stuck waiting at the dock to finish. I went back to the pumproom and adjusted the pump speed as I normally did, then slightly closed down on the tank valve for more suction.

A few minutes later, the dockworker suddenly called me and said there was a spill happening up at the plant for sure—so shut down immediately! I told him we'd just finished discharging and it was already shut off, then I closed the tank valve, turned off the cargo pump, and closed the valve at the manifold. As I guessed, apparently someone back in the storage area hadn't added up things correctly, and one of the storage tanks had overflowed and created a huge mess. He didn't tell me why over the radio, but anytime you try to put more oil into a storage tank than it holds, the outcome should be obvious.

I didn't say anything about this to the captain, and didn't log it about a shutdown due to a spill. Technically, there wasn't a spill because that's what the dockworker only claimed over the radio. And if it did occur, it was well away from the ship and went into a containment area, so wasn't my responsibility. This would've happened on the refinery's own property, and not in public waters or on public lands. I was just being the third mate after all, and minding my own business about it.

After leaving the dock, we departed for sea and steered up the coast towards the Golden Gate Bridge, heading for Martinez. This was a short run to make, and on the following afternoon at 5:00 p.m., which happened to be supper time for the crew, we arrived at the San Francisco Sea Buoy to pick up the pilot. It was normal for either the second or third mate to relieve the chief mate on the bridge so he could go back to the officer's mess and eat first. Since this happened to be my turn in our rotation—I went up and relieved him on the bridge.

After the pilot boat came alongside the ship, the pilot timed the waves and jumped up onto the pilot ladder, and then climbed aboard. This was usually a very dangerous maneuver for them to make depending on the sea conditions, as some got killed by simply boarding a ship this way. If they jumped on the pilot ladder too soon, a rolling swell may drop the ship and the pilot boat crushes the pilot. If they jump too late, they may end up in the water and have to swim around a ship's propeller. But our pilot's jump was timed to perfection, and he eventually made it up to the bridge. Also on the bridge was the captain to greet him, plus myself and the helmsman. Back in the galley, the steward's assistant was instructed to come forward to bring the menu and take food orders. This was done for the captain and the pilot, since they'd both be staying on the bridge during the whole trip in.

After arriving forward, the steward's assistant entered the bridge from the port wing and walked over to the pilot, then showed him the menu. The pilot mulled it over and finally told the assistant what he wanted to eat, then the assistant left the bridge out the same side he'd come through, and started walking aft to go back to the galley. At seeing this, the captain flew out of the bridge in his direction and disappeared from our sight. A moment later, the captain reappeared on the wing and seemed to be waiting, when the steward's assistant showed up to talk with him. Well, he didn't really get to talk much, as all the talking was coming from the captain, and it wasn't pretty. The captain proceeded to chew out the assistant for not asking him what he wanted to eat for dinner, and how it was his duty to know that. He went on and on for nearly ten minutes, slowly pulverizing the assistant with every word until he pounded him into a tenderloin.

I was startled to see the captain doing this, especially to a steward's assistant who'd come aboard the ship knowing almost nothing. Anyone can become a steward's assistant, it's the entry level position in the galley. Of all the people aboard our ship, the captain would've known this, since he became a captain by coming up through the hawse pipe himself. I lost any respect I had for this captain, because I believe he actually liked chewing out the assistant the way he did it, acting like he was a hungry shark smelling his first blood in the water.

Eventually the captain got around to telling the steward's assistant what he wanted to eat, because after leaving, the same assistant came back a few minutes later with plates of food. By this time we had gone under the Golden Gate Bridge, and were just passing by the famous Alcatraz Island. The chief mate had arrived back on the bridge to relieve me, so I left for the galley to eat dinner myself.

After supper, I stayed up and waited for when we passed by the California Maritime Academy. I wanted to see the place I graduated from while sailing by on a commercial ship again. It was somehow surreal for me in a good way, but I also wondered if the many cadets studying there knew what they were in for. I really hoped not, just as I hadn't known when I was a cadet. Better to let them have their fun before facing such a brutal industry—where companies had a hundred applicants for each available job.

Once by the academy, we went under the Carquinez Bridge, and then continued on towards the Martinez Bridge, where we were to dock the ship at the nearby refinery. The current in this section of the straits was very strong, and there was another ship already tied-up downstream of where we wanted to be. After we secured two tugs alongside us, the pilot attempted to maneuver the ship to the dock, and almost hit the bow of that other ship. I was radioing from my position at the stern how close we came to hitting her—before the pilot backed off.

Since the current was too strong to dock safely with just tugs alone, the pilot had the chief mate drop an anchor upstream, then back some chain out while the tugs swung the ship into the dock. It worked perfectly. The A/B's threw the messengers to the longshoremen and we got the mooring lines out and tightened up. After we'd finished, I heard on the walkie-talkie the chief mate ask the captain if he wanted him to bring the anchor back in. The captain said no, we'd do that later, so they secured things up forward and left the anchor out as the captain wanted.

A couple of days later we finished cargo operations and prepared to depart. I always would call down to the engine room an hour before departure and give them the "This is the Third Mate, just letting you know we are departing in an hour," notice. That way they'd have everything prepared and it was my official responsibility to do it. But while at the dock, I'd gone ashore earlier when I wasn't on watch, and it was easy to see the ship's anchor was still out when arriving back aboard.

After working on a ship for a while, crewmembers notice little things like that quite easily—maybe it's a hatch left open out on deck, or it might be something out of place sitting somewhere it shouldn't be. And just before departure, I could see the anchor was still out, but you know what, I never told the captain about that. It's true, I could've told him, but I didn't. And the reason why is he knew everything and he was the one that made every decision his way. So even though having the anchor out was wrong, I wasn't going to remind him.

When it came time to depart; as usual the pilot arrived on time ready to work. I went to my normal spot at the stern, the chief mate went forward as he usually does, and the second mate went up on the bridge. That's when I heard it over the walkie-talkie coming from the chief mate; "Oh Captain, the anchor is still out. Do you want me to bring it in now?"

There was a pause, and I wish someone had a camera on the bridge to snap a photo of the captain's face. He must have felt like a complete arse at that moment. "Uh, crap, just a second," the captain said into the walkie-talkie, and while he still held the button down, I heard him say to the pilot, "The anchor was let out when we tied up, should we bring it in now?" A moment later —"Yes Mate, start bringing in the anchor."

It was very expensive to undock a ship like this when leaving a port, since we had tugs assisting us and a pilot aboard, plus the entire crew being paid overtime. An hour delay is a pretty big cost to the company for a mistake like this one. And taking in an anchor is a very slow process already, with the windlass under power having to handle the entire weight of that anchor and chain, plus the resistance of pulling it through the mud as it grabs in deeper against the current. That makes things go extra slow.

After twenty-five minutes of trying to bring in the anchor, the pilot decided it was taking too long and wanted us to release the mooring lines into the water. Quickly we slacked them so the longshoremen could toss them off the dock, and away we were with all of our lines dragging in the water. Meanwhile, up forward —they were still slowly bringing in the anchor.

I had the A/B's with me winch in the stern lines as fast as we could, since it's a no-no to ever let any lines drag in the water like this. If the prop was to turn around and catch one, it could not only be dangerous to us, but might wrap itself up so badly that we'd lose the engines permanently.

Once we secured our stern lines safely, the pilot was able to back the ship up using the engines so the anchor came aboard faster, and after they'd secured that, they had to bring in the bow lines still dragging in the water. That all took another thirty minutes, but finally they finished and secured up forward. I happened to go up to the bridge for my regular watch, and once I arrived on the bridge—the captain was a new man.

On the way out to the San Francisco Sea Buoy, the captain must have apologized to the pilot five times about the anchor being out. And when the pilot was leaving the bridge after the pilot boat arrived, he apologized one last time, and that was that. The captain had been completely humbled by everything. I even saw the second mate in the passageway later say she couldn't believe how the captain forgot about the anchor. It was kind of a wink-wink to me and we both smiled. She'd experienced his wrath before as well.

From there we headed south and went back to Long Beach, this time to do a couple of stays for loading before heading down to the Panama Canal. The second dock was the one we'd left earlier before heading north. I was on cargo operations when the captain walked out above me on the bridge-wing with the chief mate. He was looking down at me as I was standing close to the cargo manifold, and asked me if we'd had an oil spill the last time we were at this dock. He said they were claiming it was our fault. I told the captain how the dockworker had mentioned a possible spill ashore at the storage tanks—but we were already finished discharging by then—so it wasn't our fault.

"Thank you," and with that the captain walked back to his office with the chief mate. Did I just hear him right? It was the first time he'd ever said those two words to me. Wow, I couldn't believe it. It seemed things were suddenly looking up!

After we departed Long Beach fully loaded, I was still marveling at the new radar they'd installed aboard the ship. It was a touch-screen model, and seemed three times more sensitive than the older unit. Since the ship carried two radars on the bridge, one of them was still an older model, but it was easy to notice the differences between the two. It even became more apparent the farther south along the coast we got, as the seas went flat and the new radar was able to pick up small objects that the other radar never recognized. When passing by the Bay of Tehuantepec, the new radar picked up a small boat at night displaying no lights, and as we passed by it, I went out on the bridge-wing. I could see it was a small wooden dinghy with no one inside, perhaps it had broken away recently from a large fishing boat and went missing? It was certainly nothing to stop the ship for, so I just watched as it disappeared into the darkness behind us.

On the trip through the Panama Canal, I did see an interesting thing while stationed at the stern on the way through. Up in the sky there appeared thousands of birds all flying in one direction, sort of like what you'd see in an old horror movie. I sat there wondering what they were, and then it dawned on me—they were vultures—huge black ones that were headed somewhere together across the sky. Where they were going, I had no idea, but I was glad it wasn't where we were headed.

Once out of the canal, we hit the same rough seas again heading north. I wondered if there was ever a day of calm weather in this patch of the ocean, since every time we sailed through it seemed to be blowing over twenty-five knots—with the heavy swells rolling us severely until we hit the Yucatan Channel.

Up on the bridge one evening, I went up to relieve the chief mate for my normal watch, arriving ten minutes early to check the chart and read the logbook. I also had to get my eyes accustomed to the darkness outside, and to talk with him about how the watch went. This time though, I made the big mistake of talking about things happening outside of the watch, and it would come back to bite me later.

The chief mate was very tall and had played basketball in college as a center, which meant he was the tallest player on the basketball court. Unfortunately he also happened to be a huge Boston Celtics fan—as I found out that night—even though he'd never actually brought up basketball before on the ship. I'd watched many NBA games on TV myself, including the rivalries between the Boston Celtics and the New York Nicks, Indiana Pacers, and other NBA teams.

I say unfortunately because he was talking like the Boston Celtics were so good, they should've won an NBA championship every season, despite the Los Angeles Lakers having beaten them twice in the last few years. I casually mentioned how the Lakers seemed to be the better team, and had deserved to win. And since they were from my home state—why shouldn't I think that? Uh oh, I shouldn't have. At the time I didn't realize it, but I'd just committed a horrible sin; namely, one should never question sports with superiors. Quickly I forgot about it, but the chief mate didn't. And even though he had told me I'd done an amazing job on the last run aboard this ship, none of that mattered now.

Then I found out the captain was going to be relieved in Houston when we arrived. A few times recently, he'd come up to the bridge to just sit in the captain's chair and observe things, including watching me work. The day before we arrived in Galveston, he came up during my morning watch and sat down, and while I never really tried talking with this captain before, I walked up and said how it must be nice to be going on vacation again.

No, he stated, he'd rather stay aboard the ship. He gave me no reason why—and I didn't need one. While out at sea, he was the captain, and he was important. But once he got ashore, he became a nobody, just like I was. I could see him counting the days to get back out on the ship from vacation, where he'd become the powerful captain again. He really was a captain, though, in all senses of the word. But I didn't envy him, and he almost made me feel sorry for him—just for a split second—until I came back to my senses.

After we made it to Galveston and then on to Texas City, the new captain came aboard, and it was the same one from the earlier trip as well. These two captains must be in rotation between them, I thought. We also got a couple of returning A/B's, with one of them being a very nice gentleman who was nearing retirement. When he saw me walking by out on deck, we talked, and he mentioned how he'd been sailing on this ship ever since she was first launched almost twenty-five years earlier. He brought this up to tell me how I was the first third mate ever to return in all those years, and that he was retiring as an A/B. The company was going to give him a party before he got off later. I thanked him and mentioned how he was a true seaman.

We did get another new crewmember in the galley; it was a steward's assistant that had very long fingernails. They were about a half-inch past the fingertips, and he sailed with them like that for a couple of weeks aboard the ship. So not only had I been served a cockroach earlier, but now I was served by a guy with long, dirty fingernails. It was bizarre how neither the chief steward, nor the captain, would tell this guy to cut his fingernails, and they should've told him that the first day he arrived. I bet the departing captain would've squared him away, I do have to give him credit for that one.

Since this was close to wintertime in Houston, the temperatures on deck were much cooler when it came time to working the cargo operations. There was less chance of lightning strikes, and there were even fewer mosquitoes out than we'd seen last summer. I'd gotten used to the docks where we worked by this time, and sometimes the refinery workers were allowed to come aboard and eat with us in the officer's mess. On one occasion I was talking with them, and how they all seemed to be so young for doing this type of work. One of them mentioned it's because they usually end up with cancer by the time they hit fifty years old, and by then, it's too late to cure. I wasn't sure if he was kidding or not, but I believed him. And one of the dockworkers eating with us was a chain-smoker to boot, so that couldn't have been helping matters.

After we finished discharging cargo, the chief mate came up to me and asked if I'd like to earn some extra overtime—so naturally I said yes. Then he pointed to the two drains on the main discharge lines, and said to open them up tonight and just let the liquid run out onto the deck into the closed scuppers. It should be nearly all water coming out, with only a tiny amount of oil, and would run back to be pumped away later. It sounded strange to me, but I had to believe him.

At 6:00 p.m. I went out to open the drains, and after the first one was uncapped, the water and oil came out on deck. I wondered if this was even a good idea, as it didn't look right to me. Then I went over to the other drain and started to open it up, but after a small amount of water had flowed out, I decided to stop. I capped them both off and left the main cargo deck.

When I came back out for my 8:00 p.m. watch, I saw the A/B's with the bosun out mopping up the oily sheen off the deck below the drains. The bosun asked me why I'd opened them up, since it wasn't my job. That's when I went to see the chief mate, who was conveniently sitting with the captain—and it was the captain who informed me that I'd caused an oil spill. He told me this with a smile on his face, and mentioned that I only get three oil spills with the company before I get fired, and this spill counts as one of them.

Instantly I knew what this was all about. The chief mate had gotten back at me for questioning his precious Boston Celtics while out at sea earlier, and made it so I had an oil spill on my record, even though nothing ever went into the water. I didn't argue with them though, as it would have been pointless, and I didn't feel bad about opening up the drains either. If simply dropping oil on a deck was a spill, then I'd seen enough already for the whole deck crew to be gone—meaning this wasn't anything other than immature revenge.

After I left them and went out on deck, I wondered if I should just forget about it or do something to get back at the chief mate. I knew the ship's operations very well already—how she was loaded, where every tank valve was, and what exactly was being done during our cargo watches. Maybe I could slip down during the chief mate's watch, crack open a valve, and sneak back up to my cabin undetected. But on second thought, I just laughed the whole thing off and didn't seriously consider doing it, knowing at least the A/B's had gotten some free overtime out of it.

After we shifted docks and finished loading the ship with no new problems, we headed out to sea—and got back on our regular routine of standing bridge watches again. I was glad to be away from there, while hoping this was my last trip with this chief mate. He was scheduled to get off when we hit Long Beach, so I was looking forward to that day. On one watch when I relieved him on the bridge at night, I just stood by the radar after arriving and didn't say anything. Eventually he got mad—so I pretended how I couldn't see anyone due to the darkness.

There was one person on the ship, though, who was being friendly, and it was the radio officer, who everyone always referred to as Sparks aboard the ship. He'd brought his wife on for the trip from Houston, so we discussed whatever happened to come up each night while eating dinner. His wife was interested in what medical training I had, since I was the medical officer aboard. She was disappointed to learn it only consisted of one medical class back at the academy, and some books to use for a reference. Since this was a coastal tanker, I explained that a port was usually close by if we needed one, so it wasn't like we were stuck without medical help in an emergency.

When we got to Colon, we headed in to anchor the ship and await the pilots. The captain came up on the bridge to prepare for this like he usually did. And after a couple of minutes, he asked me to go up and hoist the quarantine flag over the flying bridge. He naturally had to remind me about the time I got it wrapped around the radar antenna, so he told me to be careful. However, this time the quarantine flag went up perfectly, and I proudly said so after arriving back on the bridge. Later we passed through the Panama Canal on schedule, with the pilots taking us through. I got a chance to talk with them more, and they mentioned never having been pilots outside of Panama, and having little ship-handling experience out at sea. They seemed to be groomed just for this job, and they did it well, as we never had any problems when passing through the busy canal with them piloting our ship.

A few days after leaving Panama, I was walking up forward along the catwalk when I saw the second mate come running towards me. Not knowing what was happening, I stopped as she passed me by, and then watched as she disappeared behind me into the after-house. That was strange, I thought. I continued going up forward and went inside the mid-house to the rec room.

The chief mate came by a short while later and said we'd had a fire back aft, luckily it was only an electrical fire, and they'd gotten it out before any real flames had started. That's what the second mate was running too? You would think when she saw me, she'd have said, "We have a fire back aft, come along with me." But instead she just ran past me and said nothing. I thought of bringing it up with her, but in my subconscious I heard the words; "Quick, go call the Third Mate. Hurry!" during the next emergency. And it's not like I wouldn't fight a fire, as I'd gone through a firefighting course on Treasure Island by San Francisco—where they had simulators with real oil fires and how to put them out. We practiced using foam to smother a few fires, and also how to use a spray nozzle to keep any heat away from us. But I never brought this electrical fire up with the second mate, and instead just forgot about it. She was technically the safety officer aboard, so that was her department after all. I was just glad we didn't have a real fire to put out, because those are usually deadly aboard an oil tanker.

In Long Beach we had more crew changes happening; the basketball chief mate was being relieved, with the new one already aboard to replace him. The radio officer also left with his wife and was replaced through their union. To our surprise, the new one arrived wearing a woman's hat of all things. Was he crazy? I wondered what was he thinking, but on most ships the radio officer seemed a bit nutty, and this new guy fit that description much better than the one getting off.

The shipping industry at this point was still trying to get rid of the radio operators to save on costs, so the company had asked all the deck officers to get their Marine Radio Operators Permits from the FCC. These would allow us to become licensed radio operators ourselves, and so, in theory, if all the mates on a ship carried them, then having an independent radio operator aboard wouldn't be necessary. The radio officers that the ships carried were paid very well and were unionized, so they were fighting this attempt by the company to eliminate their jobs, and had been successful so far at stopping it.

During our next meal in port, I was talking with the new radio officer and happened to mention how the last one had brought his wife aboard. When he asked me what were his chances of doing the same thing, I told him I couldn't see why not, he only had to ask the captain about it.

When we shifted to the next dock and after they'd gotten the gangway out, the first person to leave the ship was the new radio officer, who was also referred to as Sparks in the maritime tradition. He was leaving wearing that woman's hat again, and out on the bridge-wing, the captain and pilot were watching him. All the captain did was look at the pilot and say the two words—radio officer—and that was enough to explain it. The reason Sparks had left in such a hurry became obvious, when two days later his wife came aboard and they both thanked me profusely for mentioning she could sail with us. She told me she'd never been on a ship with her husband before, and so this was a treat to get to see him working aboard with the crew. She was a school teacher out on her winter break, so it was pure luck in the timing of things. And it was nice to have someone else to talk with at dinner; they were very friendly and very much in love with each other.

After finishing cargo and departing, there was a scheduling change; instead of heading in under the Golden Gate Bridge and going to Martinez, we continued sailing farther north and went up to Portland. The second mate lived in the area and so she asked me if I'd stand her cargo watch during the day—while she goes ashore with her friends—then she'd make up for it by standing my next watch at sea. At the time I wasn't thinking so I agreed to that, and as it happened, I stood a cargo watch that lasted eight hours long, something I'd never done before.

It wasn't that I couldn't do the job for eight hours, rather it was all the walking that one does when handling the tasks of discharging. That involved reading the tanks constantly and going down into the pumproom a number of times since the pumpman wasn't with us. I couldn't trust an A/B to handle the pumps after what I'd seen aboard, and the trip up and down was a workout all by itself. Try that ten times to check on pumps and turn valves, and it gets exhausting pretty quickly. By the time the eight hours were up, I was cooked, but not until after leaving port did I realize by how much. My legs were so sore I could barely walk for a couple of days, and it was like they were filled up with strawberry pudding.

This was also the watch I stood with a newer A/B who'd replaced the last one in Long Beach. The new guy was a military veteran, and I completely respected him for that, but for some reason he claimed I was born with a silver spoon in my mouth—and he said that to me before walking away in the afternoon. I knew he'd been shot in combat and had also been drafted, so maybe he felt I was privileged somehow. What he didn't know was I'd survived living in Mexico for a year with a poor family as an exchange student, and had gone to a poor school without knowing any Spanish. While that can't compare to the horrors he went though, it wasn't like I'd never gone anywhere and faced the consequences. Still, I never let what he said affect things aboard the ship, at least that's how I handled it.

From Portland we sailed out and headed to Long Beach, this time to load the ship for the trip to Houston. By then my legs had recovered enough to handle cargo operations again, since when loading I wouldn't need to enter the pumproom and go up and down those long flights of ladders. Instead, it was mostly standing around the tanks that were being topped off, and opening or closing valves on deck with the assistance of an A/B. The loading diagram showed the quantities of lube oils to load, and everything went smoothly for the crew. The second mate got off here and was replaced in the rotation.

Once we finished and were out to sea fully-loaded, we headed south again, this time for Panama. After a day out of port I couldn't believe it when the new chief mate came and asked me if there were any tampons in the medical locker. She apparently forgot to pack any when coming aboard, and now that we'd left for sea, she remembered about it too late. When I checked the medical locker—there was everything inside, including condoms—but no tampons, which meant she had to make it to the next port without them. I did put a suggestion into the medical log to add tampons for future trips though, so hopefully the company updated the inventory for any forgetful female crewmembers.

By chance I happened to go back by the galley one day in-between meals, as many of us aboard occasionally did. They had snacks and a refrigerator with some things in it for those who might have missed a meal by chance and were still hungry. When walking by the kitchen, I saw the cook making all of our salads for the next dinner. He had them bunched together on the table behind the counter where we ordered. Suddenly he let out a huge sneeze without covering his face, and it went all over the entire group of salad bowls with lettuce inside. I could actually see the spray cover everything, it was so big, and that meant no more salads for me to eat.

The rest of the trip south to Panama was uneventful, and finally we arrived in Balboa harbor. Once we anchored in the designated area, we went on anchor watch as we always did. That involved just one mate on the bridge to keep an eye on the ship's position using radar—so as to monitor if the ship drags an anchor or breaks away due to weather. As I was standing my anchor watch on the bridge during the morning, I heard a call on the marine radio for our ship. It was from another ship that was anchored nearby, and he wanted to know if we were in distress. *In distress?* I asked why he thought that and he said our U.S. flag at the stern was flying upside down, which is a maritime signal for distress. I told him to wait a moment while I checked, and sure enough, the ordinary seaman had raised it like that after we'd anchored. I thanked him and said it was all a mistake, and we both laughed. Then I called the chief mate and told her about it, which she didn't believe.

When the pilots came aboard to take us through the Panama Canal, a British officer came along with them to check all of our safety equipment. He'd been hired by the company and was scheduled to stay with us until we hit Texas City, where his report on the condition of the ship would be finished. As we started through the canal, he was already quickly getting to work, checking all of the fire extinguishers, fire hoses, axes and other safety equipment in the enclosed spaces. After we passed through the canal, he continued on and eventually got around to checking the medical locker, where he told me I was doing a sloppy job of things. I was suppose to be removing and destroying every medication that had reached its expiration date, regardless if we'd received any replacements or not. He then went through the entire inventory and took out all the ones which he deemed expired. He checked how I was logging things and didn't like that either.

When we had our next lifeboat drill at sea, the safety officer videotaped it for training purposes and also taped a fire drill we held using the equipment on the cargo deck. That was the first time we'd done that, so the crew was a bit rusty. However the captain was proud of this fact, thinking the crew did such a stellar job that the videos would be used for training purposes on all of the ships in the company's fleet. I kind of chuckled when I heard that one.

When we made our way through the Yucatan Channel, the currents were the strongest we'd ever seen, and pushed us well east of our track-line towards Cuba. During the two watches prior to my arrival on the bridge, we'd drifted nearly twenty miles off course, and the captain came up to the bridge, then had us steer ten degrees more westerly to make up for the current. Even with that, it took more than one watch to get us back on the track-line again and away from Cuba.

We also picked up another visitor while at sea, but this one was a small falcon which decided to use our ship as its hunting platform. I noticed it would perch up at the top of the forward mast by the running light, and fly off from there to catch a bird. It then brought the bird back to the mast and ate it while perched at the top. This went on for a few days as we got closer to Texas, until it saw a ship passing on our port side and flew over to join that ship, using it for a southern run. That was a real sea bird, but who'd ever believe a falcon could be that smart?

By chance while on watch, I'd gotten distracted and stayed in the chart room too long, and when I came out there was a ship dead ahead of us at two miles crossing to starboard. The new A/B and the older helmsman were both inside the bridge, and I couldn't believe a ship was so near us without either of them saying anything. Two miles at sea might seem a long ways off, but it's actually quite close. With both our ships at full speed, that means a collision between us is possible in less than four minutes. I asked the new A/B why he didn't report it since he's the lookout. He somehow thought I'd already seen it, so I told him to never assume anything and report every ship from now on. The helmsman only smiled, but after this I never trusted either of the two A/B's again.

We made it safely into Texas City and docked at the same refinery as on earlier trips. After we started discharging the lube oils, I got word that we'd be loading a new cargo later—something which the ship had never carried before—but that was all they told me. I didn't think too much of it though, how much different could it be from the lube oils?

The safety officer had finished his inspections and had left the ship, so I was glad to see him go. Even though what he did was very important and benefited the crew, he was overly British to us all, and acted like our ship wasn't good enough compared to the ones from his own country. That was the impression he gave us, it was like we couldn't wipe ourselves in the bathroom the right way without his safety instructions.

Meanwhile, I needed the rest of this trip to go smoothly as I was getting off in a few weeks, and was already planning my vacation time in my head—almost pretending like I was there already. *Just one last port to go,* I kept telling myself. When we shifted docks to finish the discharge, it was just that much closer, until one funny thing happened when the dockworker came aboard and told me he needed hourly readings from the tanks for his logbook. I told the dockworker that there was only myself and one A/B on watch, and there's no way we could do hourly readings of all the cargo tanks, including all the calculations of the cargo quantities, just for him. But he insisted, and so I told him flat out that there's no way I'm going to do it. Then he threatened me by saying if I wasn't doing it by the next hour, he'd have to come back aboard and have a talk with the captain about me.

Guessing he might be bluffing, I said we should go up and talk to the captain right now, as I wanted to hear this myself. Then he backed off, saying it wasn't necessary to see him after all—but maybe later, then he walked off the ship and went back to his office on the dock. So I'd guessed right, he was bluffing. This was the first time someone from the dock had ever asked me for hourly readings before, and no doubt this guy must be new. But I bet he didn't try bluffing another ship like that after having to eat his own words.

Despite things like this, I still enjoyed loading and discharging the lube oils while sailing aboard this ship. The actual work itself was interesting to do—as it was fun and challenging. But when the captain reminded me we'd be loading a new cargo aboard for the first time, it turned out to be a cargo from hell for me, and also for the rest of the crew. Despite the ship being designed to carry lube oils, this new cargo wasn't a lube oil, it was an explosive liquid called Methyl tert-butyl ether, or MTBE for short. It was an additive to gasoline to make it even more combustible, and was as clear and thin as liquid water. It even had a smell that made our heads spin since it contained ether. If someone smelled it long enough, they might even start daydreaming like they're lost at sea somewhere, it was that strong.

Since this tanker used open sounding tubes to gauge the tank levels, we had to breath the cargo fumes constantly when loading and discharging. I found out how strong the smell of MTBE was on my first watch when we started loading a full cargo of it to take back to California—where it was destined to become a gasoline additive for all of the automobiles in the state. And while loading always seemed easier for me, this MTBE wasn't easy to work no matter what we did. Its fumes oozed out of every cargo vent and covered the deck with a continuous blanket of the stuff that put me into a light-headed dreaminess.

As the loading went along, at times I had to go up onto the catwalk to get above the fumes on deck, so as not to breath too much of it, and just to keep my head clear. But even at that, I couldn't avoid it for long, having to go back down and check the tanks as it continued loading. When it came time to top off the tanks, I had to breath the MTBE almost continuously while watching the tape readings in the sounding tubes. This stuff was so volatile, it evaporated almost instantly when it came outside into the open air. Normally the ship relied on the lube oils to keep the tanks and valves properly coated with oil, but this cargo did the opposite—it diluted any oil it came into contact with, and once it evaporated, there was no oil remaining behind to keep the metal parts of the ship protected. How the company ever thought it was a good idea to load this in a lube oil tanker made me wonder. But they must've been making a bundle of money while doing it.

At this time the ship was scheduled to take on bunkers to fuel the ship's engines, so they sent out the third assistant to start loading that during my watch on deck. As we were also loading MTBE at the same time, I could listen to the radio and keep track of what he was up to, eventually hearing him say everything was ready to the dockworker—start giving us the bunkers. But he'd forgotten to open up the main valve at the manifold, which I reminded him to do after seeing it was still closed. The dock-worker heard this on the radio and waited, then after the manifold valve was opened, they started to load the bunkers and it all went smoothly. Did I need any more excitement at this time?

We finished loading the MTBE aboard without any further problems, and prepared the ship to sail for sea. The A/B's were the ones who always drained the loading hoses after finishing, so they disconnected everything at the manifold for draining, which poured gallons of MTBE through the grates into the open collection tank underneath them. I could only wince as they did this, thinking of all the fumes they were inhaling with that pool of MTBE sloshing below their feet as they worked.

By this time I'd begun feeling a constant drowsiness in my head, but was hoping it would go away once we hit the open waters. Unfortunately, it never did. The ship had a continuous smell of MTBE everywhere—even while at sea—with fumes escaping through the tank vents and blowing back aft, then seeping into the sleeping areas, the engine room, and even inside the galley. If that smart falcon was still out here flying around, even it would take one whiff of our ship and head in the opposite direction.

After a couple of days out at sea, I noticed a few sharp pains happening in my pelvic region while walking around. Since I hadn't felt those on the ship before, I had a strong suspicion they were due to the MTBE. It was impossible to get away from the smell, even when up on the bridge. With the fumes going up into the main house, it crept into every nook and cranny it found. If a hatch was opened up somewhere, it went in. The engine room blew air into the passageways for ventilation, and it came in that way as well. The MTBE fumes were everywhere.

We made it to the anchorage at Colon, then picked up the pilots when it was our turn to enter the Panama Canal, and passed on through safely. On the Pacific side, we left the canal behind us as we headed north towards California. While on watch in the morning, I checked the weather report to see if any weather warn-ings were being broadcast, and noticed that the weather fax needed to be programmed to the proper time. We had the fax set to local time, when it needed to be set to a UTC setting, since that's how all the weather schedules were timed. At least that made sense to me.

That evening the captain came up on the bridge and he pointed me into the chart room, where he proceeded to ask me why I'd tinkered with the weather fax. I explained that it made no sense to have it set to local time—when we received the broadcasts on UTC time. He scolded me that it's not my position to determine that, and I should never mess with the navigational equipment again without asking him, then he walked off down the stairs in a huff.

But this time I actually laughed to myself about it, since this was the same captain who'd helped the basketball chief mate report that fake oil spill on me. If I had walked on the ocean, he'd still have hated me. And the second mate should have come and asked me about the weather fax instead of running to the captain about it. A vacation from this crew couldn't come soon enough.

When we finally arrived in Long Beach to discharge the MTBE, we docked the ship accordingly. My replacement wasn't suppose to show up for a few days, so I was going to continue standing watches until he arrived to relieve me. Once the dock said it was ready, the A/B's got the cargo hoses connected to the manifold and the pumpman prepared the main cargo pumps, then the chief mate began discharging the MTBE out of the cargo tanks.

All the cargo pumps we used were located down in the pump-room, except for one. That was the electric cargo pump which discharged the only segregated cargo tank aboard, and the cargo itself was the lubricant for the bearings on the pump shaft. When discharging lube oils that made perfect sense, since that's what lube oils were meant to do. But when you have something more volatile and explosive than gasoline lubricating a bearing, you can only imagine the dangers involved.

When the time came to discharge MTBE from the segregated cargo tank, the chief mate was on deck to get the electric pump running. The bearings were meant to allow a small amount of cargo to leak by as a lubricant, and this would flow out the top of the pump and into a bucket that hung just beside it. This meant the bucket would slowly fill up with cargo, and since this was MTBE being discharged, we'd have an open bucket of it hanging right beside the electric pump.

Next the chief mate showed me how to lubricate the bearings. After she started up the electric pump, you could see the MTBE coming up around the bearings quite fast, since it was a much thinner liquid than a lube oil. So the chief mate took a wrench and started to tighten down on the bearings to slow down the flow of MTBE, otherwise the overflow bucket would be filling up too fast. She tightened down a couple of turns on the bearings and it slowed down the flow to about half of what it was, then she tightened again and the volatile MTBE in the bearings started to smoke heavily. Oh crap!

Instantly I imagined the ship exploding in my face, as we had an open bucket of MTBE sitting right there between us, with the oil tanker itself being completely full of the stuff in every tank. The smoke was enough to briefly obscure the electric motor until the chief mate turned the wrench the other way—and by pure luck —the smoke disappeared before it blew us up.

Yes, it was that close!

After seeing that happen, I never adjusted the bearings on the electric pump while doing the discharge by myself. I didn't care how much cargo leaked out past the bearings, if it filled the bucket up in fifteen minutes or five minutes, the A/B on watch would dump it and keep rotating the buckets. It was better to have too much lubrication than not enough, especially since this tanker was never designed to be carrying this dangerous cargo to begin with.

The new third mate showed up and relieved me just before we'd finished discharging most of the ship. When I went up to be signed off by the captain, there were a couple of other crewmembers leaving at the same time. The captain gave us all a legal paper to sign that stated we'd never felt any illness from a cargo carried aboard the ship. *Huh?* What's this? I asked the captain about the legal paper, as it wasn't necessary when I'd signed off the last time. He told me if I didn't sign it, then I wouldn't get paid—it's as simple as that. However, at the academy we'd taken a maritime law class, and no company could refuse to pay a crewmember. Also, there was the episode on the grain supertanker where the cleaning company had put a lien on that ship for non-payment. So I knew the captain needed to pay me even if I didn't sign, but should I press it?

I decided not to do that, and the reason being was the company knew they had us over a barrel on this. If I didn't sign it, then they wouldn't hire me for the next ship, especially if I forced them to pay me with a lien. But it seemed like the company was protecting themselves due to the MTBE, and this captain went along with it. I grabbed a pen and signed the waiver, then handed it back to the captain. He paid me off and I went on my way to the airport, where I flew home and tried to recuperate from another exciting trip at sea.

9

It's Over In Drydock

After making it back home from that coastal tanker run, a couple of months passed before I spoke with the company's agent about which ship I could sail on next. It was obvious that I couldn't sail on the same tanker again, since the last trip had given me unhealthy symptoms from MTBE exposure—where my entire body was literally drying out all the time. I'd been using a vaporizer at home to get some moisture back into my lungs, and this I was running all the time while sleeping. If I was having this much trouble after only one trip with that cargo, I couldn't imagine how bad it was for the crewmembers who'd made multiple runs and were being constantly exposed to it over and over again. It wouldn't surprise me if some of them were quitting sailing altogether over their symptoms, or even keeling over and ending up in the hospital.

The agent then looked over his schedule and hinted at the possibility of a chemical tanker that was available to work. I'd heard they were ten times more complicated to load and discharge than the lube oil tankers were, but that wasn't what worried me. It was my health from chemical exposure, and that was a bigger priority for me right now. But if they paid more, actually way more, I might've been crazy enough to consider doing it. Instead, why would I work a chemical tanker for the same pay as a lube oil tanker, when the dangers were twenty times greater due to those caustic cargoes? I told the agent I'd have to pass on that chemical ship for the time being.

Then the agent offered me a crude oil tanker doing a single cargo run before heading into drydock. He made it sound like heading into drydock was something horrible, but how much worse could it be? I said that sounded fine, so he scheduled me for the crude oil tanker.

Maritime Academy Graduate

A month later I boarded that ship as third mate in Los Angeles to load and discharge a run of crude oil, then to help prepare her for drydock. To my unfortunate surprise, I met the same captain who I'd sailed with on the lube oil tanker; the one who'd chewed me out for avoiding the fishing nets, and also had me sign the MTBE waiver to get paid. The first words out of his mouth were, "What happened to you?"

I couldn't believe this was the way we're already starting out my next trip. Ironically I explained to him about being sick due to the MTBE exposure back then, and I noticed the captain wasn't looking too good himself—he probably got off the last ship for the same reason. But the captain shrugged me off about this and went on to talk about our planned voyage for the trip ahead. He said once we finished discharging here, we were sailing up to Valdez to load more crude oil, and then we'd discharge it in three different ports. Finally, we'd clean the ship's tanks out at sea, and then head into drydock. He told me where to stow my things down below, and then he dismissed me.

When I went down to place my belonging in my cabin, a second mate was leaving and advised me to take his old room instead. He said the other one had a bulkhead built against the showers of the chief mate's cabin, and when he showered very early in the morning, it would wake anyone up who was sleeping in there. So I thanked him and quickly put my belongings in his room. Just then the new second mate showed up and was looking at me like I was up to something—I told him I was just following directions.

The new second mate found out the hard way why his cabin was worse the next day. Now some may question if what I did was fair, but if the shoe was on the other foot, I'm sure the second mate would've done the same thing to me. Eventually the second mate got increasingly angry over this, as he figured out why I'd taken the other cabin. It slowly simmered in him and would come back to bite me later.

I quickly learned that discharging crude oil on this tanker was ten times easier than doing the coastal tanker with lube oils, as the chief mate here always seemed to be in the control room when we got down to the last quantities of cargo. While on the lube oil

162

tanker, I'd done the stripping, running the pumps and communicating with the dock all by myself during watches, but here the chief mate was involved in everything. That was fine with me, as I got paid the same either way, but he must have been racking up the overtime in the process, and the company was obviously allowing it.

Once we finished discharging and ballasting the ship, we sailed for sea and headed north up the coast towards Valdez. That was the same port I'd visited earlier as a cadet, and I wondered if it had changed much in five years. Obviously this time it was approaching summer up there, while when I had visited the last time, it was the dead of winter. Since we'd barely had four hours of daylight back then, it should be much warmer and brighter by comparison on this run. And I was a third mate now with all that extra responsibility, compared to being a cadet where I could goof off and still get away with it.

After we passed by the Channel Islands on the way north, we continued along the track-line laid out on the chart. This was a course farther off the coastline than the lube oil tanker followed, which at times might be within two miles of the coast along the rocky shoreline. I happened to be on watch at night when I saw a flare go off in the distance on the starboard side. Was that really a flare? It had gone up for a few seconds and then died out like a spent rocket, with its red glow slowly disappearing as it fell back down. What to do?

I quickly walked over to the radars and checked them—there was nothing being picked up. If someone in distress had just shot that flare off, they must be in an awfully tiny boat to be doing it. Since our ship was ballasted, we rode well above the waterline, meaning it was over forty feet up to the steel deck from the ocean, so even if we did find out who did it—there was little chance of them getting aboard easily in these heavy swells.

I thought of calling the captain up and telling him about the possible flare. He would've asked me where I'd seen it, and assuming he decided to go over and investigate, it would take twenty minutes to maneuver over there, and then we'd slow the ship down to look for something floating in total darkness. I could already hear him asking me over and over again, "Now where did you see that flare?" Then after a half hour of fruitless searching, we'd leave and I would get told to never do it again. Ever.

Nope. I didn't call the captain about it and we continued on. If someone was out there, a ship this size wasn't going to save them in total darkness without their vessel showing up on the radar screen. Even a ten dollar radar reflector could have changed that, then I'd have called the captain and told him we have a target that just shot a flare off—and let him decide what to do. Instead, we sailed on and I forgot about the flare, as one does with most things while at sea.

As we went by Northern California, we started to hit a large fog bank, and it was how I'd remembered this area as a cadet. But this fog bank was much thicker, and extended for a farther distance out during the summer. At times the visibility got quite low, where we might have only a quarter-mile of visibility. The radar screens were watched constantly for other ships, as they were our only eyes through the fog.

We made it up into the Gulf of Alaska, where the fog bank had already vanished, and eventually we approached Prince William Sound. This was the entrance to steer into Valdez, but since all of the Alyeska oil terminals were full, after calling into the Vessel Traffic Service operated by the U.S. Coast Guard, we maneuvered past the entrance and anchored in the designated area. The first thing I appreciated after we'd anchored was how pristine every-thing appeared to be around us—the clean ocean water, the green mountains off in the distance, and the blue sky above us.

When I looked over the side of the ship, it seemed crystal clear almost fifty feet down into the water. There wasn't anything seen swimming around the ship, but there wasn't any pollution to be seen either. This wasn't like the Houston Ship Channel, where they had floating tires, broken boards, and dark brown water everywhere. Here it was like a fresh glass of sparkling water just ready to be sipped on.

One of the A/B's aboard had brought a deep sea fishing pole and started to try his luck while we waited at anchor. I was admiring the beauty of it all, when after a couple of minutes, he surprisingly hooked a large fish. The ship was riding well out of the water, but since he had a salt water pole with a very strong line, the fish came up on the fantail even though it had fought all the way up to break loose. I'd never fished in Alaska, nor ever seen a fish like this one before, but it appeared to be some sort of a very large mackerel.

Once he unhooked it on deck, out came a knife and he started to gut the fish. Then he got a surprise—besides the entrails, there was an unhappy parasite that came out along with it. It was like a large worm that was wriggling to find someplace to hide, and our appetite sank at seeing it. No way was anyone going to eat any part of this fish, so the A/B tossed the whole thing back into the water. I didn't blame him, as this was the last place I ever expected to see a parasite living inside a fish.

A day later we got orders to weigh anchor and enter the channel. We still had good weather outside with blue skies, so visibility was excellent as we made our way in. The pilot station was located just prior to Bligh Reef, the place where the Exxon Valdez had ran aground a few years earlier due to some icebergs drifting into the shipping lanes.

When we arrived at the pilot station, the pilot had an easy time boarding our ship, and afterwards he came up to direct us into Valdez. The captain kept me on the bridge and had the second mate go to the fantail, while the chief mate went up forward to secure any tugs once we entered the Valdez Narrows. The deck gang was already busy preparing the mooring cables and winches out on the main deck. After we turned into the bay, the Alyeska oil terminal became visible off in the distance. The weather seemed even calmer inside as we maneuvered towards the loading dock.

The pilot used three tugs to push the ship around and bring our port side to the oil terminal, where the mooring cables were secured. The ship was positioned so the large connecting arms centered at the manifold, with the chief mate spotting for when this was lined up. One thing I liked about this ship over the smaller coastal tanker was how the tugboats were well below the deck line. They almost appeared to be little toys while maneuvering around a ship so large, whereas with the coastal tanker they'd be tied up at eye level, and then toot their loud whistles—which would nearly blow out our eardrums.

After we got the mooring cables secured, the terminal workers quickly placed an oil boom around the ship for safety, just in case any oil was spilled over the side—and to keep it from spreading beyond the ship and out into the surrounding waters. The chief mate had already taken out enough of the segregated ballast, so loading commenced after all preparations were finished. We watched the tanks slowly fill up from the control room gauges, and kept the trim of the vessel so she remained slightly down by the stern. When I got off watch at midnight, I couldn't believe it was still twilight outside. What a contrast to being here as a cadet when we only had four hours of sunlight for a whole day.

When I awoke the next morning—the ship was nearly half-loaded, and as the tanks got closer to being topped off, I was reminded about the different tank sensors—one for when the tanks were coming up, and the others to use when topping them off. This was all done from within the ship's control room, where a large panel with a schematic of the ship had the valve and pump controls. A green light got displayed when a valve was opened, and a red light came on when it was closed. Outside on deck, the A/B's were doing their hourly rounds with the mooring cables to make sure they kept the vessel secured to the loading platform, and also to check the main deck and cargo areas for any signs of leaking pipes. The tanks were first topped off starting with the after tanks, and then we continued topping off while moving forward. The last tanks to be finished were the number one tanks.

There was still the paperwork to finish with the terminal, the loading arms had to be disconnected, and the boom around the ship needed to be removed, but once everything was finished—the pilot prepared to get us underway. He had the mooring cables retrieved before the tugs pulled us off the dock, and since the ship was already pointing out towards the entrance to the Valdez Narrows, we left straight away from there. I was relieved by the second mate on the bridge afterwards, and went down to my cabin to get some sleep before my next bridge watch.

After we made it out of Prince William Sound, we steered a course towards Port Angeles in Washington State, and that's when we had our first crisis aboard the ship—the second mate suddenly lost his eye medication. He came up to the bridge during my watch and told me it was something for glaucoma in a worn-out little bottle, and was stored in one of the chart drawers up on top. *Huh?* I told him maybe I'd seen it, but I couldn't remember when. No, he said it's been lost and that was the only bottle of medication he had, and while I didn't say anything, I couldn't believe he'd gone to sea with only one bottle of something so important. And why wasn't it being stored in his cabin—instead of up on the bridge where others had access to it?

It turns out he found the bottle back in the trash, and blamed me for throwing it away. I didn't have any idea how it got there, thinking he may have placed it on the chart table and it rolled off, or he dropped it somewhere by accident. But I was the convenient one to blame, and this he told to the chief mate. So less than a month aboard, and I was already having issues with another crewmember. No wonder this company went through so many mates!

After we passed through the Gulf of Alaska, we headed to the Washington coast and called into the Vessel Traffic Service at the Strait of Juan de Fuca. From there we entered the inbound lane and made our way towards the pilot station at Port Angeles. I was on watch and called the captain a short distance before arriving. I had scanned the navigational chart ahead of time, checking for anything to be careful of for the trip in.

When the captain came up, he briefly looked over our position in the chart room and then came out to the bridge. He walked over to the helmsman and asked for fifteen degrees of right rudder as he gazed out towards the pilot area. I told the captain he better have another look at the chart before cutting the corner, since there's a sunken rock up ahead of us. He quickly had the helmsman hold his course while we both went back to the chart room, where I showed him the rock marked on the chart. Even though it was listed as being a whole fathom (six feet) under our draft, it was close enough to worry about, so the captain stayed inside the traffic lane. After the pilot came aboard, the captain brought up the sunken rock and how he'd almost passed over it. The pilot mentioned a buoy used to be stationed there, but they'd removed it a few years back. At least nobody made it onto the nightly news because of it.

As we were now headed to a refinery in Ferndale to do a discharge, the pilot took us past a number of small islands on the way in. This reminded me of the approach to the Houston Ship Channel, where we had many oil rigs to keep track of along the way. After we docked, the discharge went smoothly at the oil refinery, with the only oddity being the drizzle we got starting at around eleven o'clock on both nights. Maybe it was a local weather phenomenon they had in the area?

We discharged almost half of our cargo and departed, making it out with a new pilot, and taking the reverse route of how we'd entered. But we had a problem. We left with only one working radar on the bridge, and it was only available using a heads-up display, with the other radar unit being completely down. That meant we had no collision avoidance available to use on the bridge, yet out to sea we went. And while it was the captain's decision to make, even the chief mate questioned it.

Fortunately the weather on the trip down the coast was staying surprisingly good. There wasn't any of the summer fog that normally blanketed the area, and as we continued heading south, it remained clear all the way along towards California. Since we were to discharge in Richmond, that meant we'd be picking up a pilot just off the Golden Gate Bridge. According to what was printed on our chart, there were three directions from which ships could enter the pilot station—from the north, the south, or the west. We would be entering from the north at night, and I was on my bridge watch just as we were making that approach. By chance, another ship had just dropped off their pilot and was heading up in the opposite lane to us along the coast. On the radar screen I could see the other ship as she got closer on our port bow, when suddenly, at the last minute, she turned and started to cross ahead of me. Since this was happening only a dozen miles from the pilot station, why hadn't they just gone straight out to sea from the sea buoy?

If collision avoidance had been available on our radar, it would've instantly told me how close the other ship would cross ahead. Instead, the radar I had was on a heads-up display, meaning there wouldn't be enough time to get a closest point of approach by using a grease pencil. Sure, I could've marked that ship on the radar screen, and then waited enough time to see where it crosses. But if this was the worst case scenario, that wouldn't leave me enough time to react—as we were barely a few miles apart. I quickly went to the radio and called for the crossing ship to respond back on channel 16. I waited a moment and heard no response, so I called a second time and still get nothing back. Crap!

Now I had a split-second decision to make. If I called the captain up to the bridge, he wouldn't have enough time to figure this out any better than I could now. Also, if that other ship had lost steering or their helmsman was panicked while going off course, we might have a major collision at any minute. And would anyone cross a traffic separation scheme and cut off another ship like this on purpose?

I had to quickly decide the safest way to react. I knew if we stayed on our course, then all I could do was pray we wouldn't hit them. So I had the helmsman go into hand steering, and told him to give me fifteen degrees of right rudder. I'd keep turning right until it was safe to get back on course, no matter what that other ship did. And since they didn't answer my radio call and we had no collision avoidance, it was the only choice I had left.

After our ship started turning, a minute later I had the helmsman steady up on a course heading out west, and then I noticed the other ship altering course to cross behind me. So I had the helmsman give me fifteen degrees of left rudder, and we slowly swung back towards our traffic lane, and after a few minutes, we settled back in on our original course, heading into the pilot station. If only that other ship had waited an extra ten minutes before turning, all of this could've been avoided.

I called the captain and the Vessel Traffic Service on schedule, and after the captain came up to the bridge, I never mentioned the near miss with the other ship. No need to bring up something that didn't happen, as I'm sure he would've added in his two cents on why it was my fault. After we picked up the pilot, the second mate came up to the bridge and relieved me. I found out he was getting off the ship along with the captain in Richmond, so I went to my cabin below with a smile on my face, knowing I'd have a fresh start the next day.

After we docked in Richmond to discharge, some radar technicians came aboard and fixed both the radar units. I also saw the new captain coming aboard, and he happened to be about thirty-five years old. This was his first time ever sailing as a captain, and the chief mate and departing second mate knew him. The first thing they brought up was how he didn't deserve to be a captain, since the company had passed over more qualified people in the process, hinting at themselves. The second mate was almost sixty years old, while the chief mate was closer in age to the new captain. However, based on how they'd both acted lately, I'm glad neither of them got the captain's job.

Rather than listen to them, I decided to keep an open mind about the new captain, thinking at least I finally had someone different to sail with besides the old "pros" from my previous trips. And when the new second mate came aboard as a replacement, he also seemed to be a nice guy that I could get along with. We even chatted a bit about various topics, including how he'd also suffered from exposure to MTBE.

After we finished discharging crude oil in Richmond, we departed for sea in the morning. The plan was to discharge the remainder of the crude oil in Los Angeles, and then head out to sea to start cleaning tanks. Since it was my normal time to stand watch, I was up on the bridge with the captain and pilot after departing. As we headed by Alcatraz Island on the way out of San Francisco Bay, the pilot grabbed his walkie-talkie he carried with him, and had a call. He hesitated for a moment as he listened, then told the captain and me that someone had jumped off the Golden Gate Bridge. He asked us what should we do, as though we had different options. The new captain looked towards me and had the same reaction—we should keep going. If someone had jumped off the bridge, they were dead anyways, and there's no way we could drift for hours while the Coast Guard came out to search for a body.

I remembered back to when someone had jumped off the Carquinez Bridge by the California Maritime Academy, and the Coast Guard had spent over an hour looking in that tiny stretch of water. Compared to that, the waters around the Golden Gate Bridge were fifty times the surface area to cover. The pilot agreed with us and kept going, and as we sailed under the bridge, we watched from the bridge wings but saw no one in the water. At least our conscious was clear.

We dropped off the pilot and headed south along the coast, sailing through the sporadic fog along the way. One area that always concerned me was how close we came to Point Sur, which is close to the Pebble Beach golf course. The rocks jut out enough so that it was the closest point we passed on our runs, and it was too close for me. I was surprised they never had a traffic separation scheme placed on the chart to keep the ships farther off the point for safety.

Eventually we came to the traffic separation scheme that ran by the Channel Islands, so we entered the southbound lane on our track-line. I happened to be on watch as we made our way in, and off on our port beam there were some oil rigs to use as navigational markers, which were easily picked up on radar. But there was another target that wasn't an oil rig, and it was quite a ways off on our port bow ahead of us.

When using the collision avoidance system, the radar units aboard acquired targets with a toggle that we maneuvered to aim a circle over the blip on the radar screen. Once we pushed a button on the end of the toggle, that put the blip into the collision avoidance program—which then tracked and calculated how close it would come to us. Since the center of the radar screen represented our ship, if the radar blip moved straight at the center of the screen—that showed it was on a collision course.

When I acquired this target on the radar it was at a distance of ten nautical miles, and it was showing a CPA (closest point of approach) of 0.0, which indicated it was a near collision unless one of us maneuvered. With binoculars I could see it was a very large sailboat with multiple masts, and it was heading on a course crossing us from port to starboard. After a few minutes, I checked again, and it still had a CPA of 0.0. *What to do?* I never saw pilots maneuvering for sailboats, and we were inside of a traffic separation scheme after all, so the people on the sailboat must know that.

Since our ship was partly loaded, they couldn't miss seeing us unless they were completely blind, as it was sunny and clear weather, with a strong breeze blowing for sailing. I could tell they were making good speed and they were using it to cut through the water. And since our ship was well out of the water, it would be impossible to miss seeing us ahead.

As the sailboat got closer, it was apparent we'd cross very close to each other. Their bow was pointed on a track to meet us at some point, so I was thinking about steering over to starboard a bit and have it clear us along the port side. But doing that would shift us out of the traffic lane, so I figured it was better to let the sailboat change its course instead. Then when the sailboat was only a mile away, I still had a chance to come right and put the sailboat behind me, but I didn't do it. I looked again through my binoculars, and whoever bought the sailboat must've paid millions —it was the largest sailboat I'd seen on the ocean since going to Topsail in 1984.

Then I waited longer for the sailboat to turn, and nothing. I waited a minute more, and still no turn. *Are you kidding me?* When the sailboat was only a few hundred yards ahead on a certain collision course, I had the helmsman go into hand steering. I couldn't believe the sailboat still wasn't changing course. As it approached our bow, I thought of coming right to avoid a collision —but it was too late. Since our ship was partially loaded and riding high out of the water, there was less ocean to see ahead of us because the bow blocked out a large portion of it. Then I realized the sailboat wouldn't be turning, and wondered why they hadn't seen us?

There was only one explanation—nobody aboard the sailboat was on deck watching! I instantly told the helmsman to give me twenty degrees of left rudder—to get the bow moving to port. My only hope of avoiding the sailboat was to swing the bow across, and pray it makes it. As our ship started turning, the sailboat began to disappear behind the bow—and then it was completely gone! It felt like my heart had stopped beating. Flashes of who I'd just killed raced through my mind, with the sailboat likely destroyed.

I would have to quickly put the ship's engines on stop and call the captain, then we'd have to see if anyone was alive in the water. I was in shock over what was happening, and then my heart pumped a beat again when, by pure luck, the sailboat started to reappear off the starboard bow—it had barely missed getting clipped by us. It was the luckiest moment of my life. I had missed hitting it!

Just after clearing the sailboat, I had the helmsman go amidships and grabbed the blow horn. I walked out to the very end of the starboard bridge-wing, and watched the huge sailboat as it healed by us. I was looking almost straight down at it and used the blow horn to scream at whoever was aboard to see what they'd just missed. And as I'd figured, the sailboat was steering on autopilot. There was nobody on deck watching or steering, instead they were somewhere down below. I bet they never knew we had passed them by, and eventually came out on deck thinking there were no ships in the area. Never mind that they'd given me the closest call I'd ever had at sea, and nearly gave me a heart attack in the process.

We continued on and made it to the pilot station outside of Los Angeles, and surprisingly, the new captain never found out about my close call with the sailboat. Either the helmsman hadn't told the other crewmembers, or else word never got back to the captain. Not that it mattered or I was worried about him finding out, since a near collision is no worse that a miss by two miles, at least in terms of damage. But it sure made for some excitement, and really scared the hell out of me.

We finished discharging the rest of the crude oil after docking in port, and took on some new supplies for the tank cleaning we'd be doing prior to arriving at the drydock. This was going to take over a month to finish, as every cargo tank needed to be washed, then checked for missed areas of oil—and washed again if necessary.

Once we left the Port of Los Angeles, we headed out and used the northbound traffic lane to pass by the Channel islands, then headed out to sea to get beyond the territorial waters of the United States. The deck gang was busy preparing the necessary equipment to start washing the forward tanks, hauling everything up to the cargo tanks and connecting hoses with nozzles. The captain was going to have me stand bridge watches for six hours on and six hours off once we hit the designated cleaning area. The other mates would also be doing six and six watches, but would be supervising the deck gang while they cleaned the tanks.

After we exited the traffic separation scheme, we turned straight out to sea until we reached fifteen nautical miles off the California coast. This was the distance we had to stay to wash tanks, as it gave us a three mile buffer outside of U.S. territorial waters. One of the little secrets about the tanker industry was all of the oily residue being washed would be pumped into the ocean legally as we sailed off the coast, it was only a matter of over what distance we'd discharge it all within regulations.

A track-line laid out on the chart took us north, and once we got off the Oregon coast, we would continue up to the border with Washington State, where we'd turn around and headed south using the same track-line. We would continue going up and down like that until the tank cleaning was finished, and all the oily wash got discharged into the ocean. Since we were on this odd watch schedule, the steward was preparing special meals for us when we got off watch—it was meant to keep up our energy levels.

After we'd hit the new track-line, I started standing my first six hours of bridge watch, when the captain came up to say he wants to be called whenever something passes within three nautical miles. I thought that was weird, as three miles is a long distance to be worried about. So I asked back with a puzzled expression, "Three miles, you sure about that, Captain?"

"Yes, I'm sure, it's three miles." And then he left the bridge.

Now anyone who sails at sea knows when you get close enough to a port with nearby shipping lanes, you come within three nautical miles of many vessels, both large and small. I didn't want to be calling him up for every one we encountered if it's just off in the distance, so I ignored this order and never called him for any vessels, close or otherwise, expecting at some point for him to scold me. But he never did.

And unlike the last two captains I'd sailed with—they would've jumped at the chance to nail me for this—the new captain was actually the opposite, and never questioned me on why I didn't call him. He must have seen a couple of the ships we passed by during my watches, or the fishing boats that came within three miles on a few occasions. After a few days without calling him about the shipping traffic, I knew he'd never bother me about it again, as he probably realized that the less I call him, the less he had to worry about me.

At this time the U.S. Coast Guard was monitoring all vessels preparing for drydock, so they knew we'd be washing tanks and discharging wash-water that contained heavy oils over the side. Every day I started seeing a large Coast Guard plane fly over us to record what we were discharging, and I assumed they must have been checking our position relative to the coastline for legal compliance.

The washing itself was done by using long rubber hoses that had nozzles fitted at one end. These would be lowered inside the tanks in various areas, and when started, would shoot jets of hot water to clean off the exposed surfaces. As one would expect, the interior of the tanks weren't like the inside of a cardboard box. There were many strength members built into them, including cargo piping and ladders. To get them completely clean wasn't easy, as the nozzles had to be repositioned and tied off many times, then inspected after each running to be sure they were getting the inside surfaces as clean as possible. The deck gang also placed blowers over the tanks to get fresh air inside them and to dispel the musty odors for visual inspections.

When working on other ships, I had stood six hours on and six hours off for bridge watches before, but never for weeks on end like this time. And it may seem like I'd have lots of time to get plenty of sleep, yet it wasn't that easy. By the time I was relieved on the bridge by the captain, then ate something in the galley and went to my bunk, I'd get maybe five hours of sleep during the night. That left me trying to catch up after my next watch later, where even a couple of hours more sleep would still leave me tired. And this was to go on and on for however long the tank cleaning lasted.

Since I was almost entirely up on the bridge except for sleeping and eating, I was able to keep track of the tank cleaning by watching them work from my vantage point above, while also scanning for any vessel traffic out ahead. Slowly I watched as they finished cleaning the forward tanks, and one by one, they moved back to the next set of tanks—to start the process all over again. The oily wash-water was being pumped over the side through the port discharge, and it came out just above the waterline so we could see how dark it was when it hit the ocean.

Sometimes I also went to the control room after my bridge watch during the day to get the scoop on how things were progressing from the second mate. After a month of progress, I happily went down to get word when they appeared to be finished with the final tanks. But this time I didn't find the second mate in the control room, so I went out on deck and saw him lying down by the pumproom entrance and acting like he was dying. He was stretched out on his back with his arms above his head, and panting like an exhausted dog. He told me his pulse was running rapidly and he was having major heart palpitations, just like he'd had when working on other ships lately. Then he mentioned this might be his last trip as a mate because of it.

I left him there and told the chief mate about this up in his office, suggesting that he put me out on the deck watch to help finish with cleaning the tanks. Then the second mate could take my bridge watch and use that time to rest up, hopefully to get his heart under control. After talking to the captain, they agreed to do this. The chief mate also told me that after the final tank washing today, all they had left to do was clean up the equipment, pull the hoses out of the tanks, and prepare the ship to enter drydock.

So for my next scheduled watch, the second mate went up to the bridge, and I went to the control room to start working with the chief mate—but he also seemed exhausted when mentioning what things were left to do. He remembered a nozzle was still tied down in one of the tanks that needed attention, so he directed me to go out to number five tank on the port side and follow the hose down through the manhole opening. He said once I'm down the ladders at the bottom of the tank, follow the hose as it snakes along the bottom through the rib platings, then crawl to the end and find the nozzle. Just untie it and come back out, that's all there is to it. The A/B's would go down into the tank later and pull the hose out. Well, that seems easy enough. I wondered why one of the A/B's couldn't just untie it without me, but figured they must be too exhausted from working.

I left the control room and went out on deck, then started walking forward towards the manifold. As I got over to the port side, I saw the hose going into number five tank just ahead of me. I briefly looked over my shoulder and saw the second mate watching me from above on the bridge—wow, that looked strange. Next I climbed into the tank and started descending down the ladders, and as I made my way down, I could follow the hose with a flashlight, it was over sixty feet down to the bottom of the tank. From there the hose disappeared from my view as it turned under some plating—and damn, what a big tank!

Once at the tank bottom, I crossed over and reached the bend by the edge, so I stepped down and looked where the hose went, and even with the flashlight it disappeared into the darkness. They had maneuvered it along all of these small openings in the ribs that crossed under the tank, and above it was solid tank plating along its entire length—so there was no place to stand up once I entered it. It was either crawl on my belly all the way to the end of the hose, or twist into a ball and spin around, then crawl back out if I had a problem.

I got down on my stomach—and after a deep breath—I crawled through the first opening, then crawled over into the next opening. I could actually feel the ocean moving under my chest, and then realized it was the ship's hull right beneath me! The ocean water was rushing by at over ten knots, and I imagined what would happen if we suddenly had a leak in the tank—I'd be drowned like a rat almost instantly. I was only into the tiny passageway about ten feet so far, but my heart was already beating like I was running a marathon, so I better calm myself down.

I took a deep breath and thought about turning back. This was the scariest place I'd ever crawled inside aboard a ship. Here I was all alone in a dark crawlspace with little clearance and a questionable air supply, but if I backed out now and left the tank, the chief mate would wonder why I couldn't do something this simple. He did tell me the A/B's would pull the hose out after climbing down later, but I figured none of them would volunteer to untie the nozzle by themselves. Now I could see why!

After a minute of contemplating this with the ocean rushing below me, I decided there was no choice but to continue on. So I crawled on my stomach through the next opening, and then through the next one, all the time trying to keep the flashlight pointed out ahead of me. Only once did I look back with the flash-light, and quickly wish I hadn't—then I took a deep breath after almost panicking. I continued moving ahead, until I finally reached the end of the hose after what seemed like forever in that tiny space, having crawled about eighty feet entirely on my stomach.

When I found the end with the nozzle, it was tied and pointing up to hit a spot missed in an earlier washing, so I untied the knot and let it drop down. Then I made sure they could pull the hose out without the nozzle getting caught up in the steel plating nearby—no need for anyone else to suffer through this like me. Then I spun around and started to crawl out, thinking I couldn't believe how far into the tank I was. Eventually I made it back to where I'd started from, then climbed up and out onto the tank bottom. From there I crossed over and quickly climbed up the ladders and came back out on deck. How nice it was to see the sunshine and blue sky above me. I felt lucky to have gotten out of that tank alive and still be breathing.

When I went into the control room, the chief mate was over by the table with his laptop computer. He was looking at something on the tiny screen when I told him the nozzle was untied, and pretended like it was no problem. He questioned me if I'd actually made it down there, acting like he was really surprised. I casually said yes, even though inside I knew it was the ultimate bravery test for claustrophobics to try. Fortunately, that was the last nozzle left to untie, so instead he told me the next chore I had to accomplish—one that ended up being much easier.

Once all of the items on his list were finished and the equipment was retrieved, we headed in to get a pilot at the Columbia River Bar. In the meantime, everyone in the deck crew was busy handing in their overtime slips for the chief mate to sign, and they had stacks of them. It had been just over a month's worth of work to complete the tank cleaning, but it was finally finished.

After the pilot came aboard, we sailed up the Columbia River and headed straight into the drydock situated in Portland. There was no waiting around to enter it like with the Panama Canal, we went straight in and tied up inside, then the engineers shut down the ship's engines completely. As I started to gather my belongings to sign off, the silence inside my cabin was kind of creepy. There were no more creaking or rolling noises to be heard, and no more vibrating bulkheads like we're still out at sea. Instead, the only sound came from the ventilation blowers piping in fresh air—and it was barely much to hear at that.

When I signed off in the captain's office, he thanked me for helping out and keeping the second mate safe. I told him it was nothing, but was happy to have done it. This young captain seemed like a nice guy, and I hoped he would always stay that way. Maybe the other captains I'd worked with had started out like he was, and were turned into grinches after having sailed for too long. I wondered about them. Then after departing, on my taxi ride to the airport, there was a heat wave outside with the thermometer showing over ninety degrees, but I was still wearing a long sleeve shirt like we're still out at sea. *Never mind, I had no way of knowing*, I told the taxi driver.

After the plane ride home, my body took a few weeks to recover from the six hours on and off schedule I had while aboard the ship. I was still waking up at home after only five hours of sleep, almost like my body was afraid to miss another watch. Eventually it stopped happening, and after two months at home, I called up the company's agent to ask when another job might be available, only to hear back that he couldn't see anything coming up. I was told to try calling him later.

But when I called him after another month, it was the same answer—nothing was available. I wondered if he was brushing me off just like that agent did after my trip to Singapore. Then another month passed by, and after arriving back home from a trip to Yosemite, I happened to be walking into our kitchen. Someone was leaving a message by the telephone and they sounded very angry.

When I walked over to the voice recorder, it sounded just like the company's agent. After listening for a moment, it was obviously him, and he was wondering why I hadn't gone aboard the ship he'd left instructions for with a family member. He continued on asking for me to call him, but was still talking in an angry voice. Then, as I reached for the phone to respond, he hung up.

I hesitated for a moment. What should I do? During my time with the company I'd been chewed out for avoiding fishing nets, was blamed for a faked oil spill, got served a cockroach for dinner, had a near miss with a sailboat, almost had a ship explode in my face—on and on—the list kept growing in my mind. And why didn't the agent make sure I got the message about my new ship before I'd left? Yet again, I was being blamed for something out of my control.

I pulled my hand away from the telephone, and instead erased the message left by the agent. My last ship had finally sailed without me, and now I was left ashore as an ex Mate.

THE END